POLICE
AWARE

POLICE AWARE

An Everyday Diary of One of London's Boys in Blue

Keith Rogers

FIRST EDITION

Book design by Publishing Push

ISBNs
Paperback: 978-1-80227-665-7
eBook: 978-1-80227-667-1
Hardback: 978-1-80227-809-5

Dec 2022

To ~~Michelle~~ Helen

To my amazing Cats whisker,
Let's carry on with our good work,
Solving (missing) cases, loving cute
kittens and keeping us all safe.

Love you,
Steph xx

Introduction

In 2017 I finally retired from the Metropolitan Police after just over 30 years of service. I remember very clearly having my job interview at Paddington Green Police Station back at the start of 1987 and feeling like a rabbit caught in the headlights. One thing that does stand out about that interview was being asked what I'd do if I saw a burglar climbing out of a window. 'Well, I'd grab him,' I said.

'Ah,' said the very senior-looking interviewing officer, 'but what if he turned around and hit you?'

'Well,' I said, 'I'd hit him so hard, he'd not be able to get up and hit me a second time'. He gave a little smile and wrote something down on a sheet of paper in front of him.

Later that day, when we were being given the good or bad news about our futures, I was told by the civilian admin guy giving us our results that they'd written down that I was 'particularly outstanding' – I'm sure because of that one answer, not for anything else. Bet you couldn't say the same thing in an interview nowadays though!

For the last 20 of those 30+ years I've been planning on writing down what day-to-day coppering is like, for the thousands that do the job day-in-day-out.

There are certainly no boring political views expressed in here, nor any bitterness or any axe to grind. It's just showing you what officers up and down the land face in their everyday role, every time they start a shift.

Certainly nothing in here is remarkable, special, or a one-off incident. It's what most people would shy away from, but police rush towards – the thin blue line indeed.

A person's lifetime view of the police can be forged in their one and only interaction with them, be that a traffic stop, a call for their assistance, or just simply a 'hello' in the street. I always hoped I treated people how I would have liked to be treated myself – certainly I wanted people to come away with a positive view of the police; after all, I was one of them! (Unless you're a thieving scumbag, in which case I'd come down on you like a ton of bricks.)

I always tried to live by my own phrase, that you've got to have at least one good gut-wrenching laugh every day (preferably at someone else's expense) – and always remember, you never know who you're talking to!

Every time I dealt with something interesting, I'd print out a copy of the incident and file it away at home. Some gruesome, some funny, some sad, some that if you saw it acted out in a TV drama you'd say to yourself, 'that'd never happen in real life!' – always thinking I'd put them down on paper one day – well, that day is here.

Some stories might seem pretty mundane I suppose, certainly to anyone who has worn the uniform, but as I said, it's just a reflection of incidents that are repeated across the country on a daily basis.

Every one I've written about here are ones that I have been 100% directly involved in personally. None of them killed me and I got to go home at the end of every shift. Sometimes aching, bruised or cut, once with broken bones, but you know what, I wouldn't have changed the experiences for the world.

Anyway, get comfy on the toilet and enjoy...

Contents

1.

Scarred for Life

You'd think a Sunday early turn would be a nice easy shift, but think again. More often than not you're dealing with the fallout of a Saturday night, where people aren't getting in until the early hours.

A call to another 'disturbance, possibly a domestic' comes our way (I say 'our' – you're normally double-crewed in London), so it's blue lights on and within a couple of minutes we arrive at a little maisonette situated just on the edge of a large sprawling West London council estate.

I knock on the ground floor door to the flat which itself is situated up on the first floor and the door is answered by a little Korean girl, maybe in her early 20s, who's heavily scarred.

She has fresh deep scarring all over her face, her cheeks, nose, forehead, etc., and she's wearing a very loose-fitting top. I can see her chest and breasts are heavily scarred too and for a split second I stare in disbelief at her.

Her skin looks red-raw, with parts of it curled and peeling away. She must have been in absolute agony.

As I stare at her (this all takes only a fraction of a second in real time) I see coming down the stairs behind her a Korean man, roughly the same age and our eyes meet. My first words to the girl as I point to the bloke behind her are simply, 'Did he do that?'

She lowered her head slowly and nodded at the same time.

I quickly stepped inside to her left just as the man's feet touched the bottom step and I grabbed him by the scruff of his neck, spun him around and pushed him against the hallway wall. He was told in no uncertain terms that he was under arrest for GBH (grievous bodily harm) and he was cautioned while being handcuffed.

They were boyfriend and girlfriend and it transpired that during the night she had told him she wanted to end the relationship, which he obviously didn't take to very well.

She explained that while they were in bed, he had got up and gone into the kitchen. A short time later he came back into the bedroom with one of his hands in an oven glove, holding a large metal serving spoon that was glowing red-hot (he had laid it on the burning gas cooker ring in the kitchen apparently).

He had then straddled her in the bed, pinning her arms under his knees.

While she lay there defenceless, he held onto her throat effectively pinning her head to the bed and had run the edge of the red-hot serving spoon across every single part of the skin on her face and then using the flat side of the spoon, he had run it all over her chest – a case of 'if I can't have you, no one will'. Once this ordeal had finished for her, she hadn't rung the police straight away, but had sat in the flat probably with her head spinning as to what to do, while in absolute agony. At some point she had found the courage to ring 999 and I had turned up.

Later that morning I took a statement from one of the ambulance crew that had come to the flat and she said it was the deepest burn scars she had ever seen on a living person.

I don't normally take an interest in what people receive as a sentence at court; you'll find out why later (If you always did try and find out, you'd resign pretty quickly in despair) but this bloke got 4 years for what he did. Out in two I'd guess then.

And thinking what he had done to that poor girl, how he'd changed her life maybe forever, it makes you want to weep.

2.

Coughing Your Lungs Up

Who would have thought that phrase that we sometimes use is true?

I went to a call to a 'collapse behind locked doors,' which is general job speak for any call where someone can't get any answer from the person within, or maybe they just haven't been seen for some time and friends or neighbours are worried.

There was certainly no answer and the neighbour who called us assured us the single man who lived there never went out. A check with neighbours, etc., revealed that no one had a key to his house, so a deftly aimed kick to the front door where the lock was situated had it bursting open. (It's surprising how many times this causes very minimal damage if it's just the Yale lock securing the door. More often than not you can search the house for a screwdriver and do a pretty good repair yourself so the door can shut securely.)

I walked into the living room and then the toilet (you wouldn't believe the amount of people who die on the toilet – ask Elvis) and then the bedroom.

There lying in bed was the elderly gent, sitting up on several pillows.

There was blood all over his hands, over the bed covers and by the side of his bed was an orange bucket, with a large amount of blood in it.

His mouth was wide open and hanging out of it was one of his lungs, or the lining of one of them, that went down past his chin almost to his chest.

Believe me, images like that sear themselves into your brain forever.

The scene looked so horrific, the WPC I was with took one look through the crack of the bedroom door and point blank refused to set foot inside the room. (She later became one of my governors and a damn fine one at that.)

Not unusually, an ambulance had been called at the same time as the police and speaking to one of the crew once they had turned up, he said to me, 'You know the phrase 'coughing your lungs up', well that's exactly what he's done there'.

He had a history of lung cancer and at some point, while lying there in bed, he had coughed so violently one of, or part of, his lungs had become detached and started choking him. He had simply (or not so simply) reached in and pulled it up and out of his mouth and died, probably from suffocation or loss of blood.

Not a good way to go. There's not a lot of dignity in death.

3.

Degloving

There was a flat in London that had made the news once when its occupant needed to go to hospital, but he was so obese, he couldn't physically get out of his front door. The Fire Brigade and Council had worked together and had taken out his front second floor window and using a small cherry picker crane, had loaded him onto this through the window and lowered him down to the ground.

Fast forward a couple of years and I get called to his flat when neighbours started noticing a foul smell coming from the inside.

After (again) forcing the front door (you'd be amazed how many times you'd do this; my record was 5 times in 5 days), the stench of rotting flesh hits you full in the face. Once smelt, never forgotten.

He was lying face up on his living room floor and by the look of him he'd been there quite a few days at least. He was still such a huge size I knew he'd never fit into one of those black body bags that the undertakers bring with them in their private ambulances when they move the deceased to a mortuary.

I called a friend in our control room and told them to explain this guy's size to the Coroner's Officer, so he could pass the message on to the undertakers.

Anyway, they duly arrive and of course they're stumped at the size of him and how best to remove him.

I knew that there was building work going on nearby, so I went and managed to scrounge a large tarpaulin from them and a roll of silver coloured gaffer tape. The plan was to roll him onto the spread-out tarp and secure the ends 'Christmas cracker' style with the gaffer tape.

The plan was working, but he was so big and slightly sunken into the floor, that he was never going to roll. So we made the decision to pull him onto it and as I pulled his arm, all the flesh – skin, fat and muscle – came off in my hands, basically degloving him. Yes, it was gross.

After a bit of toing and froing, we managed to get him onto the tarp and duly taped up each end.

It took an almighty effort by us to get him down the 4 sets of stairs between us on the second floor and the car park outside, with one of us going behind with a mop and bucket clearing up his bodily fluids as they seeped out the end of the tarp.

That wasn't the end of it though, as the private ambulance was designed to take four bodies, so there was a central divider in the back of it – two bodies on top, two below. He just wasn't going to fit in there, such was his size.

Another neighbour was spoken to and we borrowed a socket and ratchet set, and took apart this central divider and lowered it to the floor. At last he was inside and we apologised to the neighbours for the unorthodox way he was removed, explaining it was the only way.

Out of interest, in the gent's flat he had several scrapbooks with newspaper stories about himself – in his younger days he'd been a professional athlete. Who'd have ever thought it? I suppose none of us know how we're going to end up, eh?

I think this was the only time I ever got home and completely undressed outside before going indoors!

4.

Where's the Blood?

Yet another call to a domestic that this time had the words 'female stabbed' thrown in for good measure.

You go to some calls that come out simply as 'a disturbance' and it could be anything from a murder to adult brothers arguing because one has hidden the others' slippers. (True story! You'd like to knock their heads together sometimes, but this is apparently frowned upon.)

Anyway, back to the 'female stabbed'. The door was answered by a youngish woman who had all the hallmarks of a regular drug user (or abuser), sunken eyes, greying skin, the odd missing tooth and looking a lot older than she probably was. But she had the most bizarre injury.

She had indeed been stabbed, in the throat, and as she lifted her head up slightly to show me, I swear I could see all the way to the back of her throat. The strange thing was – no blood? It was just a massively nasty open stab wound that had me completely stumped. She said 'He's still in here,' and as we came in, a man ran past behind her, out the back door and into the garden.

We piled in (there were 4 of us who had arrived) and after clambering over and through (unintentionally) a couple of garden fences, he was caught in a neighbour's back garden and nicked by one of the others for attempted murder.

I never did find out the cause of the lack of blood; I can only assume it was some hour's old and she had cleaned it up. Still…?

5.

Broken Finger Rapist

I was asked to go to a flat in Acton, West London, to try and arrest a Nigerian man for a rape that had occurred down in Sussex.

Intelligence checks by Sussex Police had revealed his address and I attended there with a colleague who was new to the team, who had just finished his Street Duties training (where you do 10 weeks learning the ropes with experienced officers at your police station once you leave Hendon).

Anyway, after parking around the corner (I didn't want to give the game away too soon) we saw the flat was up on the first floor. Getting in through the communal front door was easy, but his flat was across a small landing, with a few steps leading down, then a few more leading back up to his front door.

This made it easy to see if there was any movement inside, as you could crouch down and watch the strip of daylight underneath the bottom of the front door. While I watched this strip of daylight, I got my colleague to knock on the door. There was no sound or movement inside, so I called out his name and said we were the police and to open the door.

With this, I saw a flash of shadow under the door, but still no reply to the request to open up. The threat of us forcing the door got no response either, so a heavy kick saw the frame splinter and the door fly open.

Directly in front of me across the other side of the flat was an open window, and a large portly Nigerian gent was swiftly climbing out of it.

I ran forward and grabbed hold of him, seeing straight away that not only was he climbing out of his first floor window to escape, but that below him was a basement flat courtyard, so in effect he was actually two floors up, not just the one.

I tried to pull him inside, but his weight was already taken by gravity and he slipped from my grasp. His feet hit a black metal drainpipe and he flipped end over end and hit the concrete ground two floors below with a hefty thump.

As I was running outside to get around the back, I called for an ambulance and those that heard me calling on the radio said it was the one and only time they had ever heard a slight hint of panic or urgency in my voice.

That caused a few other friends of mine to drop what they were doing and come to my aid without being asked, and luckily I found the bloke dazed but conscious and amazingly suffering it seemed from no broken bones or serious injury.

The same could not be said of me though and I realised that as I was grabbing him to stop him from falling, his weight had bent my fingers backwards against his concrete window sill, breaking the bones in them.

We both ended up in the same hospital, where I nicked him on suspicion of rape. I think he was discharged before me too!

6.

Life's a Bitch, eh?

Patrolling a large council estate near Hounslow at the end of a night duty, a friend and I came across a white Ford Escort XR3i (highly desirable back then) with every single window and light smashed on it.

Someone had gone to town on it with a hammer or a baseball bat it seemed.

A quick check on the Police National Computer showed it was actually parked outside the owner's address. Best contact the owner then, let him know what's gone on and try and help as best we can.

I knocked on the front door and the door opened ever so slightly enough to see an older Indian lady stood behind it.

I apologised for disturbing her and asked if the owner of the XR3i was in.

She closed the door, only for it to be flung wide open with her very irate son standing there demanding to know why police were at his front door, how he hates the police and why would we come to his house etc, etc…very anti-police.

I stood back and to the side and extended my arm to show him his car, in the style of a TV host showing a prize.

His jaw hit the ground and his eyes bulged out of his head. He didn't say a word.

The guy walked down to his car behind me and was still staring at his beloved car, arms still outstretched and eyes agog.

I walked back to our police car and got in it as my friend started the engine.

The guy stared at me and I simply said, 'Life's a bitch huh?'

As the words 'huh' left my lips, my friend floored it and off we went.

Some people get exactly what they deserve.

Didn't hear another word on the matter.

7.

An Unnecessary Suicide

I've heard many people, when talking of those who commit suicide, especially in a public setting, about how 'selfish' they can be.

What people often fail to see though, is the fact that the vast majority of the times it's not selfishness, but acute mental anguish and, for want of a better word, illness. They can be so mentally 'broken' that they're not always responsible for their own actions.

We just can't fathom the levels of pain these people are sometimes going through.

I took a call once from a husband, who had found his wife hanging in their garage. It was one of the saddest incidents I've ever been to.

This lady, some years previously in her marriage, had had an affair and was convinced she had contracted HIV.

She had carried this burden with her for years in her marriage and at this stage of her life she had two small children now too.

She had convinced herself, through deep guilt, that she had given HIV to her children and her husband, as well as herself.

One night while lying in bed, when everyone's demons are at their worst, the burden and guilt of this had become too much for her and something had snapped inside her mind. She had written a suicide note, gone out to the garage and using a length of rope, had hung herself on the garage roof rafters.

Her poor husband, who wondered where she had gone in the morning, searched the house for her and found her hanging in the garage.

Heart achingly sad, especially for the children who were around two and four years old.

And of course, subsequent medical checks revealed she did not have HIV at all. It was all in her poor tortured mind.

As an aside to this story, we used to have a creepy FME (Force Medical Examiner – basically an on-call doctor who attended incidents when requested by the police).

He was the sort of doctor who would ask a female victim of crime with, say, a black eye to take her top off, etc. Some people, officers, did make complaints about him, but where they led to I don't know. Anyway, he attended this call and when I went out to the garage, I caught him looking up the poor woman's skirt. He quickly stopped what he was doing and looked a bit flustered. The dirty old perv.

8.

Mind Your Head

Flying along once to a call with a friend, we crested a low bridge and in the distance we both saw a car parked by the kerb, with the boot open. We only had the blue lights on, no sirens at that stage, as they're not always required every second of every journey.

Looking into the boot was the owner, rummaging around for something no doubt. As we quickly closed the gap between us, the driver said, 'Watch this' and as we were just about level with him, he put on the two-tones, which obviously are loud.

In the split second we flew by, I saw the poor chap jump up with fright, bang his head on the boot lock, grab his head and bend back down in pain to where he was before. All this in a micro fraction of a second.

God I nearly died laughing; in fact I laughed so much I couldn't get out of the car when we arrived at the call. I think I cried tears of laughter for a week after. Unlike the poor guy whose head we had hurt, which was certainly not our intention. I really wish I could say sorry to him now!

9.

Knocked Down

Sitting in the canteen late one night duty, a call came out on the radio about a robbery happening right there and then. Now, contrary to popular belief these days, coppers live for this sort of call; that and a good 'suspects-on' (where there's a burglary with suspects still inside).

Refs (what we call our grub – short for 'refreshments', an age-old-fashioned term, but we like it) went up in the air, we ran like crazy down two flights of stairs, into the area car and we were off. Further info was received en route, the venue was a huge warehouse that was owned by a massive well-known mobile phone company and the security guard was on the phone to police, giving a running commentary on what was going on. I knew the warehouse anyway, so knew exactly where to go.

We must have arrived within two or three minutes of receiving the call and myself and my colleague were first to arrive on scene. It was like a scene from a Hollywood film. The gates to the warehouse had been rammed open by what we later discovered to be a stolen blue Ford Transit that was still sat just inside the gate, the scene was floodlit by all the yard lighting and mobile phone boxes were scattered all around.

I could see masked figures running around and we parked just so we blocked the entrance. It was the one and only time in my entire service that I called for 'urgent assistance' (the most important message to ever be put across the radio) before even getting out of the car.

I leapt out of the car and drew my baton, knowing that things were about to get deadly serious. At exactly the same time, I saw the suspects, all wearing full-face balaclavas, leap into an Audi S2 and the engine roared.

I locked eyes with the driver who was also wearing a balaclava, raised my baton, deciding to try and smash his windscreen. He floored it and went to drive out, but steered towards me in an attempt to knock me down.

I leapt out of the way (I decided I wanted to keep my legs) but of course I was stood right by the transit van so couldn't jump very far at all, and as I leapt out of the way he managed to strike me a glancing blow across my right leg as he squeezed by the police car and accelerated away, chased by other officers who were just arriving.

I got up straight away, to see one of the suspects had been left behind and was running full pelt out of the entrance. I ran after him, with no pain in my leg at all. Believe it or not, I was running after him down a road called Chase Road, up in NW10!

I wasn't catching up, what with wearing boots, body armour, etc., and it was at this time I noticed a good friend close behind me and another running on the other side of the road from me, all chasing down this robbery suspect.

I was calling him a few choice words and he suddenly stopped and turned to face me. He pulled off his full-face balaclava and his gloves and threw them onto the ground, then he raised what appeared to be a weapon at me and put it into his shoulder, taking aim. I didn't stop running and closed the gap between us very quickly indeed. I raised my baton and shouted at the top of my voice for him to 'Get down'. This he did and I saw the weapon was a large long handled crowbar (or 'jemmy' as some like to call them).

I shouted for him to stay down and he did. He didn't say a word as I flipped him onto his front and handcuffed him to the rear.

At this point I could feel a bit of pain in my right leg and felt a sense of relief that I wasn't that badly hurt at all. I tapped the suspect twice on his shoulder and asked, 'Are you alright mate?'

He replied that he was, and I told him he was under arrest for robbery, etc. He was detained, no longer a threat, so it was time to bring the aggression levels down a peg or two.

During the trip back to custody, we had a conversation, as you sometimes do with those you've arrested. It's not always a hate-filled experience. They know getting nicked is an occupational hazard and you've just done your job of stopping them committing their crimes and detaining them.

'It's a good job you didn't block him in,' he said. 'He's got a loaded Beretta in the glovebox and he would have shot you'.

He also went on to explain they had done another similar job out in the Home Counties somewhere and that they had outrun the police helicopter. Bit of bragging I thought, but I was later told by one of the officers investigating, that it was indeed true. Maybe it was running low on fuel and they had to terminate the pursuit. 'Blimey, not a bad boast though,' I thought.

Anyway, he did a bit of plea-bargaining in the subsequent investigation and told police where there was a lorry full of stolen kit, which ended up being recovered. He never gave names of those he was with that night.

The driver was never caught, well not for this job anyway. But some time later, the guy who we thought might have been the driver was arrested for another job and when he appeared in court outside of the Met area, he was sprung while in the box (the area of a courtroom where the suspects sit). A few of his accomplices had entered the courtroom, jumped the guards, beat them and made good their escape. What happened to them after this, I have no idea.

It took about two weeks before I could even kneel down on my right knee and play with my kids too, due to the pain and swelling, the bastards.

10.

Fatal Police Accident

One sunny afternoon I could hear on the radio that colleagues of ours on an adjoining borough were chasing a stolen car with two occupants inside.

I knew the area fairly well and knew that they were heading in our general direction. We drove towards them and at this stage they were probably about two or three miles away. So much has been written and talked about re police chases, but at the end of the day, unless it clearly putting the lives of people at risk, do you just not try and pursue them? Do you just let the criminal win? No of course not, the job of police is to prevent crime, protect life and property and, where crime has happened, to pursue the offenders and bring them to justice. Is that not how the taxpayer wants to see their money spent?

Anyhow, that's a whole other topic. Back to this chase. As we neared the area of the pursuit, we heard on the radio that the suspect car had crashed and they were calling for an ambulance.

As I arrived on scene, I could see the vehicle had rolled over during the crash and had come to rest on its wheels, facing the opposite way to the direction it had been travelling in.

The passenger side window glass was missing and the sunroof was wide open.

But lying under the car was the female passenger who had been sitting in the front during the pursuit. She had been flung out of the car during the impact and subsequent rolling over and had come to rest under the car's front offside wheel (the driver's side – come on, keep up) facing upwards.

But the way she was lying defied explanation. The front wheel was parked on her face and she lay very straight with her arms by her side, directly under the outside edge of the car, under the driver's door in effect, like she had been placed there.

The wheel was heavily pushed into her face, crushing it, with no hope of survival. The road we were in had a steep camber to it and I can clearly remember the blood flowing down to and pooling heavily in the gutter.

A few of us lifted the car and pulled her out, but there was no hope for her. A doctor had stopped to help, who just happened to be driving by. We put the woman on her side following directions of the doctor to help drain away some of the blood so CPR could possibly be started, but with no face to talk of, it was a wasted effort. She has passed away upon impact.

As for the suspect driver, I don't think I even looked at him; other officers were dealing with him. To this day I don't know if she was flung out of the passenger window or the sunroof.

No matter what she had done, she didn't deserve to end up like that.

11.

Local Hero

There was a dispute going on very late one night at one of the Traveller sites located in our borough, involving a taxi driver who had brought a couple home and they had refused to pay and walked off into one of the caravans.

Upon speaking to the taxi driver, the fee owed by them was £7 I think, not a huge amount I agree, but you think, 'How dare these people think they can just use and abuse a working man so blatantly?'

We were joined by another police vehicle and having the caravan identified by the taxi driver, I went and knocked on it. No reply as usual, but a constant knocking by me assured those inside that I wasn't going anywhere and eventually they answered the door.

Faced with the prospect of paying the man what was owed or being nicked and spending the night in the cells, the male half of the couple decided it was wiser to pay and amid all his shouting and hollering at us and the taxi driver, he produced a £10 note from his pocket.

As he was handing it over to the taxi driver, the suspect tore it in half and then put it in the hands of the driver.

The traveller turned to me and said, 'It's still money!'

I could see the taxi driver was angry, as were my colleagues, but I said to hang on a minute, as I asked the driver for the £3 change. He handed me three £1 coins and the traveller reached out his hand to accept them.

With this, I threw them across the caravan site, turned to him and said, 'It's still money!'

He blew his top, stepped forward right in my face shouting and as I pushed him backwards away from me, he fell onto his backside.

Amid all his shouting and swearing I told the taxi driver to just tape it together and the bank will accept it.

That little incident was talked about for weeks after, in a very positive fashion, even by people who weren't there that night. As I've said, some people really do get what they deserve.

12.

War Hero

Yet again, another call to a 'domestic disturbance' which could turn out to be anything when you arrive.

This one was to a flat situated on the first floor of a very neat and tidy block of flats in a leafy area of the ground (the area where any police officer works is 'your ground'). A very nice location, well for London anyway.

I knocked on the door and it was answered by a kindly looking elderly gentleman, dressed in a dark suit. He showed us inside, where sitting in a bedroom was his wife, severely injured and bleeding extremely heavily. She had multiple lacerations to her head and the amount of blood beggared belief. Other officers applied first aid to her wounds, while I requested an ambulance on the 'hurry up' (that means to come as quickly as possible).

I turned my attention to the husband and we went and sat down in the living room.

It was when he turned away from me to take a seat, I realised he was wearing a dark suit with a bright pinstripe running through it. From the front the suit appeared all one colour because of the amount of blood on it. Unbelievable.

Anyway, we sat down together and he fully explained to me in his very soft calm voice what had happened.

During the Second World War, this gentleman was truly a hero; he was very senior in what some would call 'Winston's Secret Army'.

He had written a book about his exploits and he was dressed in a suit this day, as he was going to the Channel 4 TV studies to be interviewed about the book and his truly amazing wartime work.

In this book, he had written about a famous woman who had been one of his 'students'. Nothing romantic had ever happened between them, but he had held a candle for her all these years. She had died during the war, murdered by the Nazis in Ravensbrück concentration camp. They even made a film about her. These feelings he had once held for her, he had alluded to in his book and it was a conversation about this very matter that had sparked the argument between him and his wife that day. Something had snapped inside of him and he had picked up a large heavy glass bowl and had repeatedly struck his wife about the head with it, causing the terrible injuries she had suffered.

He was offered the chance of a change of clothes and I ended up arresting him for GBH.

Once we had arrived at the custody suite and upon giving the evidence of the arrest to the Custody Sergeant (who was a friend of mine), I explained that he was indeed an elderly true war hero and that despite what had happened, he should be treated a little gentler than your average criminal. After all, he was around 80 years of age.

It wasn't long after this incident that he sadly passed away due to cancer. Despite what he had done to his wife and the injuries she had sustained, I still hope he didn't suffer too much with his illness.

I often think about him.

13.

Dogs in Boots

I had a call one night duty to a 'suspects on', at a very large Boots store in West London. A few of us arrived at about the same time and we split up, some to the back, some staying at the front.

In one of the toughened glass doors at the front entrance to the shop, there was a freshly smashed hole just big enough for someone small to have climbed through. You could tell it was fresh, as there was splintered glass all around. A request for a dog unit to assist us was met with the response of 'none available at this time'. We needed to gain access quickly and rather than smash more windows and add to the damage already caused, I asked if anyone had anything to break out all the remaining glass in the broken window. A friend driving the van said, 'I've got a big crowbar on me – don't ask why!'.

I certainly didn't, but he handed me a large crowbar and using the curved end I managed to wrench out what remained of the glass unit in the bottom of the door.

A few of us entered the shop through this now enlarged hole and as we started searching, we saw above the perfume area a hole in the ceiling, where we guessed the suspect had climbed up and into upon hearing us enter.

A loud shout of 'Police, come down' brought no response, but the ceiling started shaking as the burglar started climbing his way across the rafters. There was no way he was going to give himself up, so we decided it was only right to try and assist him in coming down to meet us.

My friend I was posted with that night and myself grabbed a couple of floor mops from the store's nice display of floor cleaning equipment and started to break off all the ceiling tiles where we thought the suspect was crawling. It was both hilarious looking back and very serious at the same time, as we all want to catch burglars – in the hierarchy of crime, there's little more important, other than murder and rape, (and maybe a little bit of armed robbery).

Anyway, there we were smashing off these flimsy ceiling tiles below where the burglar is crawling, as he clambered on all fours across the main metal structure they're attached to. (I know I said I didn't want to add to the damage already caused but come on…we're chasing burglars here!)

We follow his movements across the entire shop ceiling, breaking off ceiling tiles until we reach the fire door at the back of the shop. Here, looking through the glazing of the door, we see him crash through the ceiling onto the floor below.

At exactly this time, we were joined by a dog handler who had become available and had come to the shop. I could see by the side of the fire door the wall-mounted emergency door-release button and this was pressed, breaking the small glass panel and unlocking the fire door.

We flung the door open and the dog and his handler entered the back room to search it, and we followed behind. Just to my right as I entered, squeezed down behind one of those metal cages used to wheel stock about, I saw the burglar trying to make himself as small as he possibly could. He was curled into a ball, with his head down between his legs. Almost like a little hamster, but not quite as cute. The dog had gone right past him, missing him, which they do every once in a while.

With a loud shout of 'Got him,' I grabbed hold of him and pulled him up to his feet and was greeted by one of our regular burglars who we all knew.

Might have guessed it was him; he was only a skinny bloke and must have been in his 30s if I remember. A habitual burglar.

One in the bin (loose term for getting one in custody) for non-residential burglary…lovely.

14.

Boots Again!

And here we find ourselves back at the same Boots, one dark evening. It's obviously the shop of choice for the discerning night-time burglar.

I arrive on scene to find several officers already at the front and I ask if the back of the shop is covered. I'm told there are officers around the back, so I thought I'd go around and join them.

I run around and lo and behold, there's not a single officer there! Which was a pity, as the burglar had decided he wanted to leave and was now trying to smash the back door down.

I jump over a wall giving me direct access to the back door and call on the radio for someone to come and assist me, as I'm on my own.

Whoever is inside is still very determined to leave and they're kicking the door for all it's worth. Someone does come to assist me, but I'm met with a call of, 'I can't get over the wall!'

Oh for Christ's sake!

Right then, time for a bit of 'big boy's rules' here. He's a burglar, I'm on my own and very soon we're going to meet. Maybe there's more than one? Gloves off time.

With one almighty kick of the back door by the burglar, it flies open and he runs out, just as I run forward into him on purpose, grab him by his throat and push him hard several feet back into the shop and up hard against a wall.

He's told in no uncertain terms that he's nicked and upon orders from me, offers me his hands to handcuff, which I'm only too happy to do.

His coat is stuffed full of perfume and aftershave and he's a lad of around 19 or 20 years of age.

Now once you've gone in for a hard arrest like that, you'd be a total arse if you kept up with that attitude. Once he's detained and not a threat to you, duty of care begins.

I said to him, 'Did I scare the shit out of you doing that?'

'Yeah, you did a bit,' was his reply. After that we got along OK – he's not on my Christmas card list or anything, but the job's made easier if you can talk to the person you've arrested.

Anyway, as I say, treat people reasonably and you get so much more out of them. I made sure his handcuffs weren't too tight and he explained to me he was out nicking high value stuff just to sell on and make a bit of easy cash.

Probably to fund his little drug habit, like so many others, making people's lives a misery as they do so.

15.

Back Door Burglars

They say before you join the police, that you'll probably only ever catch a burglar in the act of burgling a house maybe once in your entire service.

Now I don't know who first ever said this, probably someone who never left the station! My best ever was 6 pukka house burglars over a 6-week period, but more on that later.

Here we are with yet another call to a 'suspects on', this time when I was out walking the beat in a not-to-salubrious area of London.

I knew I was only three roads away from the address given on the radio, so with my friend, who I was walking the beat with at the time, it was hats in our hands and we ran full pelt to the address. It was an end of terrace house, with a side and back alley – always a favourite combination with your average house burglar.

As we crept down the side alley, we could hear heavy banging noises and after sneaking a peak over the fence, we could see there were two men both with garden spades.

(They had first broken into the garden shed of the house to get tools to do their burglaries – it saves having anything incriminating on them if they're ever stopped and searched by police prior to committing their crimes.)

They had the spades wedged into the patio door and were trying for all they were worth (not a lot) to prise the UPVC door open. They had obviously been trying for a few minutes as there were gouge marks from the bottom to the top of the door, but it wouldn't yield to their efforts.

My friend and I both leapt over the garden fence in unison and rushed them before they could take a swing at us with the tools which, luckily, they didn't try to do.

In fact, they gave themselves up pretty easily, a case of, 'It's a fair cop guv, you've got me bang to rights'.

Another two burglars in the bin (a slang term for putting criminals in the cells) and a good day's work done.

16.

Infant Death (no easy way to say it)

Some things that you deal with stay with you all your life. They may not be a daily thought in your mind, but you still think of them far too often than is ever really good for you.

I reckon I've personally dealt with maybe five child deaths in my time in the job. Every one is absolutely tragic and heartbreaking for all involved, but one certainly stands head and shoulders above the others in terms of how it affected me personally.

It was a nice sunny early turn when the call came out over the radio to a body lying at the base of a big block of flats, possibly a child.

Being not too far away, I take the call and arrive first on scene. I quickly park up and at the same time, I'm looking over to the block of flats and can see something white lying in the uncut grass. I run over to it and it's immediately obvious it's a child of around the age of one or two years maximum, wearing nothing but a nappy.

He's just lying there, looking for all intents and purposes like he's asleep. A quick check reveals he's not breathing, so I get my face shield from my pocket in preparation for doing CPR. As I go to place the head in a neutral position and lift the chin, I can feel that the back of the child's head, rather than feeling firm, feels totally crushed and soft. It's obvious that he's fallen from a height and information comes out over the radio about what floor he'd fallen from. The 11th floor to be exact.

As other officers arrive, they're told to go up to the 11th floor and try and find what flat he'd come from.

Whilst all this is being done, I'm left with the child and I start doing CPR on my own, some rescue breaths to start with and a mix of these and chest compressions thereafter. Now, I'll never forget this, as I'm doing CPR, the child appears to be getting larger and stiffer, a condition I later found out from a paramedic was something to do with massive internal bleeding.

And just to compound the horrendous situation, my face shield breaks and I'm left doing the mouth-to-mouth part of the CPR skin on skin with the child. There was some bleeding coming from his mouth and to this day I can clearly remember the taste of his blood in my mouth.

It's always a relief when the ambulance arrives in these situations and it was even more so on this occasion, although they can never take over what you're doing straight away and it's always a case of 'You're doing great, carry on' while they set up their equipment.

Obviously the child had been killed by the fall. I never got to see the mother; she was dealt with by other officers and I'm sure whatever they witnessed with her that day will probably stay with them too. We've all given death messages in our time, but when they're basically nothing more than a baby, well, maybe you can imagine...

One abiding memory of this day is asking a nurse in the hospital after we had arrived there if they had anything I could clean my mouth out with as, looking up in the mirror, I could see I still had the child's blood caught up all between my teeth. I needed to phone home and speak with my wife as my own little boy then was about the same age as the little lad I'd been dealing with. I just needed to hear him.

I mentioned the further information received about what floor the child had fallen from. That info came from an elderly couple who lived in the block opposite to the one where the child lived.

I went and took a statement from them later in the day. By coincidence they had been sitting by their window looking out having breakfast and had seen this child on the outside balcony of the flat where he lived. They had watched as he had climbed up onto something and had tried to climb up over the railing. As he climbed over it, he appeared to hang on to the handrail just for a second or two and then had let go, or more likely his weak grip had given way and they watched him fall to his death. That part of the story always makes the hairs on the back of my neck stand up, even now as I type this.

I hope they got over what they saw...well, better than I did anyway.

Police leave incidents, but some incidents never leave the police.

17.

Laughing Until My Face Hurt

It's not always doom and gloom in the job, many's the day I laughed so much, I literally had to hold onto my cheekbones they were aching so much from laughter.

One time was on a night duty when I was operator (the dead weight who sits in the passenger seat) on the station van, with a very good friend who was driving, and was known for having a bit of a short fuse when it came to some of our 'customers'.

We drove towards a lad who was sitting on the kerb late at night, with his head in his hands, on the driver's side of the road. My friend slowed to a stop and asked, 'Are you alright mate?'

No reply was forthcoming from the lad, so my friend asked again. Still no reply and with this I could see my friend's fuse getting shorter and shorter. 'Talk to me then,' he asked, in a slightly louder tone, but this still didn't get the reaction he was after.

Now this really got my friend annoyed, after all he was only trying to see if he was OK and not in need of any help.

So, raising his voice to that just below a shout and leaning forward, he goes, 'I'm talkin...' WHACK!!

He had smacked his head hard against his closed door window! He'd forgotten to open it! No wonder the lad didn't respond; he couldn't hear him because my mate was trying to speak to him with his window wound up. I think I cried tears of laughter for a month. Or was it a year?

That brings me onto another thing that's stuck in my mind for years. We're part of a shield serial (for riots, etc) and up in central London for a demonstration of some kind. I'm sitting in the middle of the carrier, which is basically a long wheelbase Mercedes Sprinter van, by the sliding side door. A friend is driving and he pulls up by the side of an officer on horseback, a friend of his from the mounted branch.

My friend who is driving simply says to his friend on horseback, 'Hiya John', to which some wit sat in the back of the carrier says, 'How do you know that horse's name?' I cried tears of laughter. Sounds so simple to say it now, but I still laugh about it now more than 25 years later!

Oh, and another – a friend who could never stay awake on a night duty (or a day shift come to think of it), was sound asleep in his grub break in the canteen on a night duty. We thought it only right that we should turn on the TV, put it on to an 'adult' late night channel, put the remote into his hands and leave him there for someone else to discover! Little things please little minds and all that… also like farting into a large clear plastic property bag and then quickly putting it over someone's head and holding them down. Cue tears of laughter from all who witnessed it.

One night duty I found, chucked in a skip, an old computer screen and keyboard. Everyone has a look in a skip when they go past don't they? Just me then…

I thought of a good use for it and took it back to the office in the police station and set it up on a desk and left it there. Come the end of the shift when we're all in there writing up reports of one kind or another, I'm sat at this mock computer set up I've made and I pretend to start getting angry at the screen, whereupon I pull out my truncheon and commence to smash the keyboard and screen to bits. I'll never forget everyone's reaction, a mixture of horror, shock and surprise.

It's not uncommon to do the odd wind-up on a new probationer, but some are just a bit more streetwise than others. We were called once to a body floating down the Thames, so a friend of mine commandeered a small boat and its owner, no more than a canoe with a small motor attached really, and went out and took hold of the now rather bloated body. He dragged the unfortunate soul back to the edge, where we lifted him out onto the side. I explained to the new probationer with us that he had to have a good look inside the mouth of the deceased and to make a note of fillings etc. – 'FUCK OFF with that!' he says, 'you're winding me up'. Never did get him; he was far too savvy.

I could go on and on here; the PC who was on a shield carrier attending the Labour Party conference in Brighton, turning up with a kit bag with his riot gear in and attached to the bag was a kiddie's bucket and spade and under his arm he had a beach ball! Again, I laughed for weeks about this one.

Nicking your friend's warrant card and sticking a picture of Homer Simpson or whoever in it and seeing how long they used it before realising, a PC walking accidently into a newly laid thick concrete path like from some old black and white comedy film, filling a PC's car with loads of dead wasps hanging from thread from the ceiling after you learn he's got a wasp phobia (I wasn't directly responsible for that one, but I wish I was) and filling the same PC's locker with dozens of wheel trims from cars, because he comes from Liverpool and, well, you know! Just wanted to make him feel at home with some stolen car parts! The WPC who'd nicked some totally naked bloke for smashing up a bar and when she was walking him out of there, she was holding a towel in front of him to preserve his dignity, but she was holding it a bit of a distance away and having a good look with a smile across her face that stretched from ear to ear! Oh and of course the frantic phone call I received from a newish lad on the team, who was on a cordon at a murder scene. He had been having a smoke and flicking away his fag ends, when the SOCO (the Scenes of Crime Officer who does all the forensic evidence gathering) had arrived to do her thing and had picked up some of his cigarette ends and was bagging them as evidence at the scene!

We had another chap join our team, who was forcibly moved from the police traffic department where he had been for many years, as he had been there too long the management thought, and it was time he moved on. Some would say that's an unwise thing to do to certain officers in specialist roles, as he really knew his stuff, even sat on the British Board of this-and-that, and all those years and years of knowledge, in effect, went to waste. Anyway, he ended up with an office job at the station, and one night to make him feel at home there a few of us, whilst out on our night duty patrols, collected so many car parts from skips and scrap sites, we managed to build him a car around his desk, complete with doors, wings, wheels, a windscreen, and even a couple of old door mirrors! He thought it was great, unlike the office manager apparently, who had a sense of humour failure.

One of the finest wind-ups I've had the pleasure of being part of was when I was the actual 'victim' of it, so to speak. I know, 'How dare they?' I hear you shout!

It was a November day, and I had to get off on time on this particular 12 hour long shift, as the wife and I had arranged a night out, starting with going to a big fireworks display in a nearby village. It's a yearly tradition. I had been telling a very good friend who I was posted with this day about my plans, and how no matter what, we had to finish on time. Maybe I mentioned it once too often. It was while I was in the police station gym smashing out a circuit (on my grub break) that he hatched his plan to make me think I'm going to be late off, after explaining it to other team members in the canteen, who were all up for being in on it. So while I'm training, they get into my locker, and wind my watch forward an hour, along with the time on my mobile phone. They also got my car keys, and put the clock forward in my car too. Not content with that, they put forward every clock in the station, including the clock in the armoury. Everyone was in on it, from the PCs to the Sergeants, all the control room staff and even my Inspector.

Anyway, towards the end of the shift, a call comes out that goes unanswered. My friend I was with knew I couldn't ignore the call, it's not in me to do that, so through gritted teeth I accepted the call and made my way, all the time no doubt complaining about how we'll be late off. Others were attending the call too, just not saying so on the radio, so I'd think it was just us going to it. Unknown to me, the radio call was all staged. So as we arrive, and start searching for something that obviously didn't exist, I'm watching the minutes tick by and thinking, after all my plans, I'm going to be late off after all. One of the other units who turn up eventually say they'll take over at the scene so I can get away. Woohoo! I make it back to the station, thinking I'm only about 10 minutes late off. As I'm booking my guns in, the Armourer (who is also in on the wind-up) says, 'Blimey, you're well late!'

'I know,' I say, as I'm chucking various rifles, pistols and Tasers at him.

I finally get in my car, thinking I'm the last one off on this particular shift, drive home as quickly as possible (ahem) only for the wife to appear surprised and say, 'Why are you home so early?' I check my watch and see I'm more than an hour late. I looked at the clock in the living room, which showed the correct time, and I must admit I was totally stumped for a while.

'I'm late,' I say, but the wife assures me I'm home very early.

Now I'm even more confused. I try to ring my friend but he doesn't reply. I called another friend and as she answered I asked her what the time was. No reply to that, just her crying with laughter so much she couldn't speak. In the background I can hear others yelling and laughing their socks off. Then I suddenly have that light bulb moment, the penny drops, and everything becomes clear. I say what a blinding wind up it was, and thank them for getting me and my friend away early from work; that's a plus in anyone's book.

A few of us have an app on our phones that show where we are. I open it up to find my friend is still at work. Then it becomes clear who the main perpetrator is! Awesome work by everyone involved there.

But you know what? Even though I was home well early, I still somehow mixed up the fireworks timing and arrived late, missing them completely!

Amid all the crime and death, you've got to find time for a laugh (especially the sort where your cheekbones ache so much from laughter!)

18.

Fits Like a Glove

Yet another terribly sad suicide and this one was an adult male who had leapt to his death from the top of a large tower block.

It was a tower block police used to get called to all the time and wasn't somewhere you went alone. More than once police had been lured there on some fake call only to be jumped and assaulted, or have some heavy object thrown from the roof onto their car. We even had an officer shot there but he lived to tell the tale. Oh what fun the estate occupants used to have! (Also, where we used to park our cars when coming into work, officers came back to their cars after a shift to find headlights smashed, or wheel nuts loosened, or syringes or razors taped under door handles, etc…absolute scum some people.)

Anyway, the place where this guy landed had very high kerbstones and it was on to one of these he had landed head first, from the 12th floor.

The remains of this guy's head and brains covered a wide area and also a few nearby parked cars. Now what made this one interesting(?), was the shape of what was left of him.

He had come down right on the edge of a kerbstone and all that was left of his head was the very bottom part of the jaw and just a part of the back of his head. If you had offered him up to the large kerb, what was left would have fitted around the kerb like a glove, or two pieces of a jigsaw. He basically had a large right angle cut out of his head, leaving only that bottom part and the very back. It was a truly strange sight and, as I've said previously, if you had seen this in a film, you'd have said, 'That could never happen like that in real life'. Yet, happen it does.

Incidentally, it was a friend and myself who had the job of going around to the deceased's mother and breaking the awful news to her.

(Now, in my view you don't just send any officer to do a death message. When I had my stints in the control room, I only sent the most mature, empathetic and caring officers to do this job.)

Upon telling her the most tragic news she's ever going to hear in her lifetime, she wheels around her living room and crashes down onto her dining table, breaking it in half. Not the most extreme reaction I've heard of, two friends doing a death message once had the recipient have a heart attack in front of them!

19.

Everyone Needs a Bit of Luck

I took a call late one night to a female who had been sexually assaulted in a car by two men, raped in a house, then driven away and just dumped outside a tube station. Apart from giving the name of the tube station to the 999 operator, the poor girl hadn't a clue where she was.

A colleague and I turned up and we sat her in the back of our car. We sat her on top of a brown paper evidence bag, just in case any 'evidence' was lost and gently began to ask her about her ordeal, showing as much care and compassion as we could, for she was understandably incredibly upset. This was no doubt a life-changing incident for her.

She began to explain to us how she had been out with friends and had managed to get separated from them and had taken up the offer of a lift from two men who had been in a club with her. Once in the car with them though, their true intentions had come to light and they had both taken turns in sexually assaulting her as they drove around and eventually stopped at a house where she was marched inside, raped, bundled back in the car, then driven away and just dumped out on the main road where we were now.

She said that she thought the car was a black VW Polo and she clearly remembered that the raised part of the floor between the back seats' footwells, where there was an ashtray, was piled high with cigarette butts and ash. She also remembered a large sticker in the car's side window.

I asked her if she could see anything around her when she was looking out of the car, or nearby where the house she had been taken to was, and she said she saw the blue and yellow sign of an Ikea store.

Knowing there was one only a couple of miles up the road, I got the map out and saw that there were maybe half a dozen roads around there where she could possibly have seen the shop from.

I asked if she minded having a quick drive around with us before we took her to a police station that had the facilities to better investigate this sort of truly shocking crime and she thankfully agreed.

In the very first road we pulled into and stopped in, I saw a black VW Polo parked a bit further up than us. It had a large sticker in the side window – it couldn't be could it? I parked up some distance away and wandered over to it. There was no one around at this late hour and upon shining my torch into the car, I saw that in the area between the rear footwells there was a pile of cigarette ends and ash.

Bingo!

We drove out of the road, parked up and explained the situation to my control room. A plain clothes unit was sent our way to watch the vehicle in case anyone came back to it, along with a couple of marked cars parked a couple of corners away.

I took the girl to a police station where she could now be properly looked after and evidence could be obtained. It's never a pleasant ordeal for the poor unfortunate victim, but there's no other way of securing evidence in the hope of a conviction at court.

This was one of those jobs where everything went right, for a couple of hours later two men emerged from a nearby house and they both got into the VW Polo. They were then stopped and both were arrested for kidnap and rape.

I can't say what the final outcome of this was as you just go onto the next job and then the next job…it's never ending.

I truly hope the girl managed to recover from her terrible ordeal and has somehow come to terms with what she went through – never get over it, but just be able to live as normal a life as is possible. I wish her nothing but the best in life.

20.

Still Smokin' Hot

Now no one likes a paedophile, but at the end of the day they have to live somewhere ('As long as it's not near me,' I hear you all say, including myself) and this particular paedophile was housed, after doing his time following a conviction, on the third floor of a large, dark-brick-coloured dreary-looking tower block, one of two built side by side on a local estate.

We had a call one day saying his front door and hallway had been set alight and, upon a swift race to the flat, the flames had been extinguished by a valiant effort from both himself and his neighbours. An amount of accelerant, which turned out to be petrol, had been poured through his letterbox and over the front door and set alight.

Doing the usual round of immediate house-to-house enquiries (or rather flat-to-flat enquiries in this instance) a neighbour told me they knew who'd done it. When they were coming home at the time all this was happening, they saw a local chap they knew walking out of the block carrying a large green petrol can. They told me he lived in the block just opposite and although they didn't want to get involved with providing an evidential statement or anything, they were happy to point out his flat to me and provided me with a brief description of him, down to the beanie-style hat he'd been wearing at the time.

A couple of us went over to the other block, up a few floors in the lift (don't ever touch the lift walls with your bare hands, they're as much a toilet as they are a means of vertical travel) and I went and knocked at the flat that we thought matched the one this witness had pointed out to us.

It was answered by a chap who fitted the description very well, apart from the hat. What he did have though was a magnificent head of hair, in the shape of a beanie hat, where all the hair below where the hat had been was all burnt hair, even his eyebrows were heavily singed!

And just to top it off, there just by his feet where he stood in his hallway was a green petrol can and you could smell the petrol heavily in the air. Honestly, it was hilarious (apart from the arson with intent to endanger life, which is what I nicked him for!)

He fully admitted what he'd done; in fact, he seemed quite proud of it! He said he knew the guy living there was a paedophile and was 'just giving him what he deserved'. And the arsonist got what he deserved: 18 months inside – he put the lives of everyone who was in that tower block in danger by setting it alight.

21.

Overtime Robbing Robbers

I was tasked once with taking a new probationer out with me, showing them the ground and generally giving them a good bit of schooling in policing and how to go about doing the job in general. It was their very first day out 'on the streets', so I was keeping everything slow and methodical and answering all of their questions.

We had just driven onto a road in a trading estate I knew well, early in the afternoon, and I was explaining to them how this was a good area for patrolling around at night, as it was one of the largest trading estates in the UK and a favourite with your night-time burglar.

As we drove towards the end of the road to turn around, a call came out over the radio, not from my control room, but an automated alarm call (the type of alarm given to people who are extremely vulnerable and at a high risk of attack or robbery in their homes or businesses) – it's normally hanging on a cord around their neck, or a push button activation type thing on a self-contained radio unit, I think.

Anyway, a person deemed at high risk of attack had pressed their alarm and by pure chance we were right outside the business address the radio call had stated, literally within 20 feet of it. I stopped quickly, leapt out and told my new colleague to follow me, also telling my control room I was TOA (time of arrival) right there and then.

I drew my baton, not knowing what I was going to come across and ran into the building, which was a single large ground floor office in a block of similar offices – dealing in what exactly I'm not too sure, but whatever it was he had people who were obviously out to get him.

There right in front of me was the business owner, being held down across a desk by two men, one of which had a knife to his throat, the other holding a large pair of scissors up above his head. Both men were shouting at him and hadn't realised I had entered to start with I think.

Once again it's gloves off time and certainly no time for niceties. I ran towards them and yelled and swore at the top of my voice, swiftly telling them what would happen to them if they didn't drop the knife, etc. right away – I'm sure you can imagine. They must have shit themselves at the speed of the police response.

Now I know I say swore at them, which on the face of it doesn't sound very professional, but when you're faced with a knife-wielding suspect who has that knife to someone's throat while pinning them down, you do whatever it takes to get you into that 'ready to fight zone'. I certainly make no apologies for it whatsoever and would defend any officer who did the same until the day I die. Only when you've successfully tackled a violent suspect armed with a weapon yourself with a little, 'Excuse me sir, would you mind awfully stopping that please,' will I change my mind on this.

Anyway, they take a step backwards and luckily do drop the weapons and we arrest and handcuff them both immediately. The new officer I was with? Jumped straight in without any fear or hesitation. Awesome.

We later learned that this had been quite a large ongoing job for some time, the exact facts behind it escaping me now. What I was told was that there were various squads from London boroughs working together on this job, from Organised and Serious Crime squads, to the TSG (Territorial Support Group) and now the suspects had been caught red-handed, that was the overtime gone for them for now!

This job can go from one extreme to the other. Sometimes you're getting an old lady's pots and pans down from a high shelf on Christmas Day because she can't reach them and she's called her local police station for help – true story (I was more than happy to assist her, poor love). Other times you're nicking violent robbers in the act.

Who says there's never a police officer around when you need one?

22.

A Famous Complaint...

There are always people willing to make complaints about things you've done, or indeed not done in some instances.

Some are justified, but the majority are just made by people as a counter claim after they've been arrested or something, thinking, 'If I make a complaint, they won't take any further action'. It happens all the time and is predictable and boring.

I once had a woman make a complaint about me after I left her with a graze running down her side that was caused by my actions.

The fact was, she was threatening to jump to her death out of an open window and when she tried to do just that I grabbed hold of her and managed to drag her back inside to safety, assisted by a colleague of mine, but in doing so had rubbed her side against the window catch and this seemed a good cause for complaint!

I've had burglars I've nicked, even with the family jewellery in their pockets or hidden in the upturned bottom of their jeans, who wouldn't come quietly, make complaints for assault, when all they're doing is resisting arrest and you're making sure they resist no more.

It was one of these burglars that got me my weirdest complaint ever though.

The allegation that I had assaulted a house burglar was to be heard at my Police Area Complaints Division, so I duly attended with my Police Federation representative.

The officer who was to interview me, a Detective Sergeant, told me he had a few things to get ready first and he told me just to sit at his desk while he got things sorted.

While sitting there, I noticed his large desk diary just sat open, staring at me. Now this was too good an opportunity to miss for a bit of a prank, so I thumbed through it and clearly remember making a diary entry on the page of September 20th. Must have been the first day which was blank I reckon. It's a bit of a thing in the police, almost a tradition actually. You leave your pocketbook (your notebook that you write in) lying around somewhere, and you'll come back to find it's been 'cocked' – someone will have drawn a large cock and balls in it. Maybe not on the very next page, but in a day or two you'll be writing something down, turn the page and wallop, there it is!

Anyway, the entry I wrote read – 'Colonic irrigation, Kingston Hospital, 10am', which I thought was hilarious.

I closed the diary and thought no more of it. The interview went ahead, I gave my side of the story and that was that. Obviously, no case to answer, a burglar wouldn't come quietly, so force was used on him, but only a reasonable amount was used, just enough to detain him.

After all, we're not thugs; it's just some people will try and assault you in order to affect their escape.

Fast forward about a week and I get a phone call while I'm in bed from my Fed Rep, who's also a close friend. He asked if I wrote in the Detective Sergeant's diary and I said, 'Oh yes, that was a good one'.

He explained that they'd done some handwriting analysis on the entry (yeah right, of course they have – not) and had made an official complaint about me.

A complaint from the complaints department! No one had ever heard of that one before.

Anyway, after a while, back I went to the complaints department to be formally interviewed on tape about what I'd written. It was a Detective Chief Inspector who led the interview, accompanied by the Detective Sergeant whose diary I had written in.

I was cautioned (this was a full-on official complaint!) and the DCI opened the interview with 'When you came here to be interviewed, you refused our offer of tea and coffee – why?'

I said that I never drink tea or coffee, never have in all my life.

He then said sternly, 'And during the interview you took your tie off!'

This was getting bizarre. I turned to the DS and said, 'It was a hot day, and I asked your permission to remove my tie and you said I could'.

Then the DCI asked, 'You wrote it on the page of 20th September, pay day – why?'

'First available page I think' said I.

Then came the main cause of their complaint…

'Colonic irrigation, so you think we're full of shit, do you?'

Wow, the penny dropped then; he thought I was telling them I thought they were full of shit! That thought hadn't even crossed my mind; I had meant nothing of the sort, just a funny thing to say was all that was on my mind.

The DCI says, 'I demand an apology'.

'Well', says I, 'I'm sorry you don't have a sense of humour'.

It all went downhill after this remark, with threats of stopping my pay for two weeks etc., so discretion being the better part of valour, I duly apologised for the diary entry I had made.

What a waste of time, but I could understand now why he was annoyed. Anyway, when all that was done and dusted, I left the building, only to be stopped by the diary-owning DS outside.

'Just to let you know,' he said, 'I didn't make the complaint. I read the entry you'd made, and laughed at it. The DCI was in the same room. He asked what I'd laughed at, he read it and hit the roof!'

I was somewhat a local celebrity on the borough after that; everyone had heard about the complaint from complaints and wanted to know the full story, as it's not something you hear of every day. Hilarious!

23.

A Christmas Day Farmer

Coming in for an early turn one Christmas morning, I was crossing a busy road from the car park to the police station, when I was nearly run over by a car driving along on the wrong side of the road. I did a bit of a leap to avoid him, not really wanting to spend Christmas in A & E, as I'm sure I would have missed out on the double-time bank holiday pay.

I watched him come to a sudden halt a little bit further down the road when he saw car headlights coming towards him on the correct side of the road, blocking his path.

I jogged down to where he had come to a halt, along with a couple of friends who were also coming in to work. I opened his car door and got him to step out onto the pavement.

Now he was a strange sight, for there stood in front of me was a bloke who looked like he had just stepped out of a combine harvester on his farm.

He wore a checked shirt, an old battered wax jacket, jeans and a big pair of mud-covered boots. Even when he spoke he had a broad West Country accent. He stank of booze and on his front passenger seat was a bottle of whiskey, that was about a quarter full (or three quarters empty, depends if you're an optimist or a pessimist I suppose).

I told him that he nearly ran me over and that he was clearly pissed.

He said he wasn't and I picked up the whiskey bottle. 'What's this then,' I asked and he said, 'Ah, that was a Christmas present. I only started that on Christmas Day'.

'But it's Christmas Day today,' I explained!

I asked where he had driven from and he said he had driven all the way up from Devon, hoping to get a flight out of Heathrow.

He didn't have any bags and had no passport with him.

There was obviously much more to this than first met the eye and I asked, 'What are you running away from then?'

People don't just turn up at an airport still in their working clothes, especially if you're working out in the fields of your farm.

He replied that he wasn't running away from anything. I pointed out to him that to drive from Devon up to Heathrow on Christmas Day, with no bags or a passport, hoping to get a flight, drinking heavily, he must be running away from something. He assured me he wasn't.

And I assured him he probably was.

Anyway, I arrested him for driving whilst unfit through drink and he was walked into the nearby police station, while someone else repositioned his car.

During the 'drink drive' procedure at the station, I telephoned the local force where he had driven up from, Devon and Cornwall Police, and ended up speaking to the local area Inspector down there, trying to see if this man was indeed of any interest to them.

I gave him the gent's details and he said he'd get back to me shortly, which he did.

It just proves that your suspicions and gut instinct are normally correct, as he was indeed running away from things. That thing in question was a serious sexual assault on his young stepdaughter, something he had been arrested for only a few days before. (All sexual assaults are serious obviously, but some are 'classed' as serious rather than using the word rape.)

He had been arrested and bailed and his passport was seized, which would explain why he was trying to get a flight without one.

He was further arrested by myself for breaching his bail, one of the terms of which was to sign on daily at his local police station, something he hadn't done the day before. He was charged with the 'drink drive' offence and left to sit in the cells while officers from Devon and Cornwall had a nice little day out up to the 'big smoke' to come and get him.

So if you ever see a drunk farmer in the queue as you try and board your flight and he's not part of a stag do, think about what he might be running away from and let someone know!

24.

Shocked Taxi Driver

One early shift I had a lad who was new to our team posted out with me. He was an experienced officer and this was just his first day on a new ground, so I was just showing him around as you do. We were standing outside a branch of WHSmith in Heathrow Airport, which was my last posting before I retired from the job.

We were talking about this and that as you do, when a customer came out of the shop and said to us, 'There's a guy collapsed on the floor in there'. We ran inside and indeed there on the floor was one of the taxi drivers who stand around the arrivals area with their placards, with the passenger names on who they're there to collect.

He was fully conscious and breathing and I knelt down by his side. I called for an ambulance via my control room. They normally arrive pretty quick here, as the airport has its own ambulance station.

He was sweating heavily, holding his chest and was having trouble breathing smoothly. He told me he was having chest pains and that his chest felt tight and my first thought was, 'He's either having a heart attack, or he's about to have one. Just behind him on a shop display stand were a load of those crescent-moon-shaped pillows travellers buy to put around their necks on a long flight. I grabbed plenty of them and put them behind the man's head and back to lift him slightly off the floor and to make him that bit more comfortable. I also raised his legs to help improve his circulation.

While I was doing this, a few airport staff members had arrived and I instructed two of them to go off in different directions and find a defibrillator in case we needed one (AED – Automated External Defibrillator). There were a few dotted around here and there, some visible and some for whatever reason were hidden behind a false wall, with only a sticker on the front of it to tell you what's inside! What good is that?

While they were away doing this, I was talking to the man, getting his details from him, his wife's details, etc. and my colleague was busy writing them all down.

One of the staff members returned to me and said they'd found a defib machine but the alarm went off as they opened up the wall-mounted case, so they left it there. I told them in no uncertain terms to run back and get it right away, which they quickly did.

The man's condition seemed to be getting worse, so I told him I was going to attach him up to the defib machine just in case. I opened his shirt and attached the pads and turned the machine on ready.

Just as I was doing this he had a massive heart attack, clutching his chest wildly and became immediately unresponsive. My mate I was with attached the lead from the pads into the defib machine while I started commencing chest compressions on the poor guy.

Now I'm no paramedic, but we've all had pretty decent training in things like this and on a personal note, I think this was the 13th time in my service I had directly given CPR myself.

Other officers arrived and cleared away some of the people who were having a nosey as to what was going on, making sure an ambulance was en route and just confirming our exact location to the control room, etc.

The defib talks to you and advises whether you should carry on doing CPR, or to wait while it analyses the patient. After another round of chest compressions, it advised a shock should be delivered.

Making sure we were clear of the man and not connected by anything in any way, I called 'clear' and I pressed the button on the defib and gave him his first shock.

Now we've all seen in films when people are shocked in this way and the body convulses upwards – let me assure you this is definitely the case in real life also. After the machine quickly made another analysis, it said to continue with chest compressions, which I started doing again. Chest compressions aren't like on TV where the chest is hardly compressed at all and with good reason. You've got to compress the ribs down so far that they literally squeeze the heart, causing blood to pump around the body. I've done it twice in the past when I've heard a rib or two crack, especially on older people.

We ended up shocking him a second time and continued with yet more chest compressions. At this stage a single paramedic arrived, shortly followed by an ambulance crew and when they were set up and ready we were able to take a small step back and leave it to the professionals. No more shocks or CPR were required anyway; he had his pulse back.

The paramedic that had turned up first said to me, after analysing the man's readouts on his equipment, that the heart attack had been so severe, that if he hadn't had the defib already attached to him, the chances are he would have died. Wow, good decision there then.

In good time the patient was placed into the back of the ambulance and, with me following in the car, we set off for Harefield Heart Hospital.

Now this is something that I'll never forget, because as we pulled up at the hospital, there was a whole surgical team waiting for him on the outside steps.

He was wheeled inside and I followed on behind. I thought we were still in the entrance foyer, but no, just behind this external door is where the life-saving surgery takes place. What was strange, was that the man was fully conscious and staring me straight in the eyes. I gave him a thumbs up and he gave me a brief sign of acknowledgment.

I was shown into a small side room by one of the staff, where there were a bank of screens showing all of the man's blood vessels and arteries. One of the staff pointed out to me a solid area of white on the screen and said that this is the blockage that caused his heart attack. I watched as a thin tube of some kind was fed up his artery and seemed to open the blockage right up. I'm sure anyone with a medical background could explain this much more clearly and accurately, but to my eyes that's just what happened, the blockage just disappeared as if it was being sucked away.

We left the hospital, completely in awe of what the NHS could do. God, they really deserve every penny they earn and more.

It was a week or so later when I thought I'd check up on the condition of the poor chap and what amazed me was this had happened on a Saturday and he had been discharged home on the Tuesday. Lucky number 13 for me I guess!

I never heard from him again, but all in all it was a good day's work.

Talking about luck, I took another call at the airport to a male who had suffered a cardiac arrest. He had been travelling with his wife and after they had landed they were going along one of these 'travelators', basically a flat escalator to speed up the long walk between gates.

While walking on this, he had suffered a heart attack (It's quite eye opening to witness the amount of people who suffer serious heart problems, or indeed pass away while flying. You'd be surprised.) and had fallen backwards, quite literally into the arms of a group of heart doctors who had been travelling back from some medical convention in Switzerland. When I arrived, he was already hooked up to a defibrillator, surrounded by doctors, and had his pulse restored and lived to tell the tale I'm pleased to say.

Once again, if you watched that on a TV show, you'd think the bounds of probability were being stretched somewhat, but it's all true!

25.

Machete Wielding Madness

Hot days certainly can affect people's behaviour; you definitely get a lot more calls and they can have a tendency to be of the more violent type. Of course this can be down to the fact that more people are out and about on nice sunny days, but on these days you know there's always going to be trouble brewing somewhere.

I was part of a shield serial (a group normally comprised of a sergeant and maybe six PCs equipped for dealing with disorder, riots, etc.) tasked with covering a big fair in a large town out in East London, near Dagenham.

Whilst your radios are normally set to the channel dedicated to the main event you're policing, there's always a couple of you who have the radios set to the local borough channel, just in case you can lend a hand somewhere else, especially if an interesting or much more urgent call should come out. After all, you wouldn't want to hear of some serious incident happening and you were around the corner from it and didn't know about it or have the opportunity to help.

And then the call comes out on the local radio link, to an ambulance crew being attacked by a man wielding a machete. 'That'll do for us,' we said.

We put ourselves up for the call and the driver races to the estate where this is happening, which as luck would have it is a short distance from the area we were tasked to patrol.

As we drive onto the estate, we can see an ambulance parked up in the distance and accelerate up to it, stopping a short distance behind it.

I slide open the side door of our carrier and leap out just as two ambulance crew run very fast around the corner just in front of their ambulance. They see us and shout, 'He's coming behind us and he's got a knife!'.

I drew my baton and ran around the corner to be confronted by a shirtless man about 30 years of age. He had long hair and a dirty long beard and was running towards me with both his hands in the air, clutching hold of the biggest machete I had ever seen, screaming.

I remember clearly holding my left arm out and raising my baton up with my right hand, shouting at the top of my voice, 'Stand still, stand still', ready to deliver a mighty blow to him if he didn't stop.

But stop he did. I shouted at him to drop the 'knife' and as luck would have it he did this too.

I shouted, 'Get down, get down' and again he did so.

As I went forward to handcuff him, thinking I must have looked pretty formidable to him, I glanced behind to find all my crew there standing right behind me, all with their batons drawn ready to protect the ambulance crew and ourselves. Got to love a proper team effort.

Anyway, he's arrested by myself for possession of an offensive weapon and affray and maybe even threats to kill if memory serves me correctly. While we were back at an East London police station writing up our notes, my friend said to me, 'Why'd you say everything twice then, everything twice then?' Got to love a bit of piss-taking haven't you!

26.

Smashing up a Shell

Night time always seems to bring out the more, 'how shall I say it?' 'juicy' calls. A friend of mine and I sometimes talk about how one set of nights, (that'd be seven night duties in a row) we were posted on the area car together (the primary vehicle that would ideally be despatched to the most urgent calls in the first instance) and we were first on scene at and dealt with three murders and four fatal car accidents in that one block of seven shifts. Or was it four murders and three fatal car accidents? We can never remember correctly.

Busy times indeed.

Anyway, this particular night duty shift was no exception. A call had come out to a vehicle driving into a Shell petrol station and by into, I mean through the garage shop front doors and into the shop itself.

As I arrived on scene, I was greeted by a camper van parked at an angle on the garage forecourt and a group of Australians who had been inside the van, all sat on top of the driver of the car that had crashed into the garage shop.

The front of the garage building was totally wrecked, with doors, window frames and broken glass lying strewn around the front.

Inside was even worse. There parked up almost on its side was a black BMW, wedged up against the various shop display stands that it had gathered up underneath it as it was reversed at high speed into the shop area. There was building framework lying everywhere, with loads more smashed glass and the shops stock scattered as if a bomb had gone off in there.

Speaking with the garage cashier who had been working there at the time, the BMW driver had filled his car with fuel and had actually come into the shop area, he presumed to pay for it. The cashier had seen him putting items from the shop display into the inside of his coat and had challenged him about it. There had been a bit of a heated exchange between them and the driver had left the shop without paying for the fuel, and gone back to his car, followed a short way behind by the cashier, who at this stage had picked up a tin of something from the shop display in his hand.

The driver got into his car, had started the engine and was just driving away, when the cashier hurled the tin at the car and smashed its back windscreen.

(You can certainly understand his frustration, as when we used to deal with 'drive-outs' as they were called, when drivers would just fill up with fuel and drive off, either in stolen cars or cars with altered registration plates, the cashiers in the garages would explain to us that the amount stolen was often deducted from their wages. Seemed a very unfair practice to me.)

The driver, I'd guess incensed at this damage caused to his car, put his car in reverse and while the cashier was standing by the shop entrance doors, he had reversed at high speed and with no hint of stopping had rammed the garage doors. He had continued going through right into the inside as his car flipped up nearly onto its side and became wedged on all the store displays.

The cashier had managed to leap out of the way just in time. The driver had then tried to run away, but had been grabbed by the camper vans occupants and pinned down while one of them called 999.

I'd only ever seen a car 100% crashed fully into a shop once before and that was someone who, doing a three-point turn, had hit the accelerator instead of the brake and had parked her car nicely slap bang into the centre of a clothing shop. That was on a night duty too luckily, so no customers were in there!

The driver by now had been stood up onto his feet by colleagues and was already handcuffed. After I had spoken with the cashier, I arrested the driver for Attempted GBH, Dangerous Driving, Theft, Criminal Damage and Drink Driving. A nice little assortment of offences.

And if memory serves me correctly, I think all in all he got about a year in prison for his efforts.

27.

Nowt So Queer As Folk

It always amazes me what people do to themselves or others, or their general attitudes to things, without any thought or reflection on their own behaviour.

For example, one of the first disasters I was posted to was the Clapham rail crash at the end of December 1988. Here, being only a probationer myself back then, I was posted to a cordon on the periphery of the crash, only to end up turning various families away from the scene, as they were just turning up, just to 'have a look and show the kids' – unbelievable.

One time I nicked a man on an international arrest warrant for the murder of his aunt some time previously. While I was giving the evidence of the arrest to the custody sergeant (a process where he decides if the arrest was justified before he books them in) I explained that the man I had nicked had murdered his aunt, stabbing her 79 times.

I was corrected on this by the suspect, who was most affronted by what I had said. 'I only stabbed her 76 times,' he said. Does that mean he was counting?

I took a call one day to the sounds of a baby crying that had been going on all morning according to the lady who called us, who was a new mother herself. The crying was coming from her attached next-door-neighbours house, which we could all hear, but I couldn't get any answer at the front door. Thinking the occupier may have collapsed, or the child had been left alone, I smashed a window in the front door, reached in and opened it. Inside was a stereo playing a tape of the sounds of a baby crying, on repeat it appeared, with the speakers pressed up hard against the adjoining wall of the neighbour who had called us.

Obviously he had had enough of the new mother's baby crying and thought he'd dish out some 'see how you like it' punishment on her.

I got his door boarded up and I was later told he had contacted police furious at what we'd done. But at the end of the day, that one was down to him.

Another was a call to a random male acting strange in a supermarket. When we arrived I was confronted by this man with blood dripping down from his mouth, chewing away on something, just making unintelligible groaning and moaning sounds. He wouldn't engage with us at all and then opened his mouth wide to us and we saw he had a mouth full of razor blades, just chewing away on them. We weren't too far from one of the West London Mental Health clinics, so it was fair to assume he may well have come from there.

The first thing is now we'd turned up, it was down to us, the police, to look after the welfare of this guy, duty of care and all that. Quite right too, for as soon as we started dealing with him, he was effectively now under our care and control. First thing that flashed through my mind was that if he swallowed these razors, what would that do to his insides? His mouth looked cut to ribbons and he was bleeding more and more heavily it seemed. The first duty of police is to save life and limb. Only one thing for it, I grabbed him, and taking his legs from under him, put him on the floor with me on top of him.

Using my extendable baton, I prised his jaw open and along with my colleague, we managed, after one hell of a lot of struggling and wrestling, to get the razors out of his mouth. He was detained under the Mental Health Act and was sectioned for his own safety after a spell in A & E.

Anyone who's done it will tell you, being stuck in hospital with either a prisoner or someone who is mentally ill and aggressive is a morally sapping experience, where every minute seems to last an hour. And it's never a quick experience either.

Of course some are amusing too, like the lady and her boyfriend who came to the front counter of the police station. She was stuck in a pair of handcuffs used for their bedroom exploits and they sheepishly came in asking to borrow a key. And of course they weren't your usual police type handcuffs, so our keys wouldn't fit in the hole. With the Fire Station almost across the road, we got them to pop over and they were freed with some specialist cutting gear. Were the couple embarrassed? You bet they were, but of course we played it down for them!

I won't mention the night-time security guard we caught 'pleasuring himself' while we looked through the windows of a large car dealership one night duty. I'll never forget the look of shock on his face when he saw us though, hilarious!

Then there are the drink drives; the legal limit is 35 micrograms of alcohol per 100 millilitres of breath. My highest blown by a prisoner after an arrest was by a woman I stopped because she was driving at high speed while her small child stood up between the front seats. She blew 165!

And the Irish guy I managed to stop as the camper van he was driving was swerving all over the road. As I opened his driver's door, he literally fell out onto the road and lay there. Once in custody, the sergeant thought I was winding him up when I said he'd been driving; he refused to believe me at first!

Once I was dealing with a robbery, where a group of lads and girls, all aged around 18-ish and from Kensington and about the same size as me, had been robbed of their phones by a single lad who had threatened them with being stabbed if they didn't hand them over. No knife had been seen, but they all handed over their phones and the lad had run off towards one of the estates. A few of us turned up for this and after identifying a couple of the victims who could best describe the suspect, I put them in the back of my car and drove around the nearby estate to see if they could see the lad who had robbed them. One of the girls, without any hint of humour or irony in her voice, said, 'Ooh, is this where all the poor people live?' And she meant it. Different lifestyles…

28.

Your Heart Bleeds

Every now and then, you end up dealing with people whose whole world can be crumbling around them, in the most heartbreaking of ways. It's so important to recognise this straight away and act and deal with them accordingly. 'What if the boot were on the other foot?' you must always think. 'What would I want done for me?'

I once had to meet a gentleman off a flight at Heathrow, whose poor wife was down in hospital in Cornwall and she was being kept alive just long enough, they hoped, for him to make his way there to say his goodbyes. Can you even start to comprehend what might be going through his mind? I can't. Calls like that stay with you; you never forget them. I certainly don't.

It was our job to meet him off the flight at the door of the aircraft, bypass immigration (this could all be done on the phone), put him in our car and blue-light him all the way down to a motorway service station down in Dorset. We had made contact via my control room with Devon and Cornwall Police and had arranged to meet them at the halfway point, which was this service station in Dorset, and transfer him from our vehicle to theirs once we arrived.

Our leg of the journey went ok, I just hope that the other half of his journey was just as smooth and he managed to say his goodbyes.

Christ, it breaks your heart, doesn't it?

29.

Hung Himself

Another one that has always tugged at my heartstrings was the plight of a poor guy who had decided to take his own life. The details are firmly etched in my mind, even his full name which of course I shan't reveal here.

He was in fear of losing his job due to a shake-up at his place of work, where he had been for over 20 years. Another thing that had compounded how he felt, was a visit from the senior management of his company, only to be asked by them who he was. He spoke of all this in his suicide note.

Sure he was to lose his job and the financial security that this afforded him and his family, and the thought of not getting other employment due to his age, his tortured mind had snapped and he had decided to hang himself.

He had gone to his place of work in the early hours one morning, laid out many photographs of all his family around him, along with his suicide note and hung himself.

I was first on scene yet again, along with a good friend of mine. It was clear he had passed away and using a knife we carefully cut him down, cutting above the knot to preserve any evidence. We had been joined by a crew from the London Fire Brigade and between us, as I cut him down, we took his weight and laid him very gently onto the ground. We couldn't leave him hanging where he was, as due to the location (which I won't mention out of respect for the family) he was clearly visible to many people.

At the Coroner's Court, sometime after, it was agreed it was death by suicide. A very sad incident for all concerned. I often think of the guy who had to go and break the news to the gentlemen's wife and family. I think it was one of his colleagues, a friend of the family as opposed to a police officer.

Maybe it was better that way.

30.

Get Down

The usual call to the night-time town centre fight comes out on the radio and it's to a Kentucky Fried Chicken shop, where some guy is said to be fighting with staff. As we drive up and get out, I can see the clear plastic screen that separates staff from the customers (sometimes a good thing) is split and broken and the cash till is lying broken on the floor.

The staff say, 'He's gone down the road,' and as I look up, I can see a guy that, due to his body language, appears to be 'squaring up' to start a fight with another group. We get back in the car and shoot down the road to them. The suspect has obviously left them alone, as they're back walking seemingly unconcerned down the High Street, but then in an area set back from the road, just where the shops have a bit more pavement width outside compared to the others, I can see our guy fighting wildly with a group of girls. They're swinging handbags and fists at him, while he's wildly striking back with blows himself, although none seem to be connecting; it's just a windmill of flailing arms.

I leap out of the passenger seat of our car and extend my baton, as I can't see this going any other way than a fight and it's sure not me who's going to lose.

As I run towards him with a view to just grabbing hold of him to stop his actions from hurting anyone, he sees me and swings a punch aimed right at my face. I duck down fast and his fist shoots above my head and at the same time I strike upwards with my baton while I'm bent down, as I'm not too keen on being punched in the face.

The baton happens to strike him across his forehead, not my intended target, it's just the part of him that I make contact with first. You certainly wouldn't take aim at someone's head for a baton strike on purpose, for obvious reasons; it's where the brain is and we want to just stop people attacking us or others, not kill them or make them suffer irrepairable brain damage.

As I come upright, I strike his knee with my baton, with a loud shout of, 'Get down!' This he does, but not due to any conscious effort on his part. He collapses to the ground, bleeding heavily out onto the pavement from his forehead.

He's unconscious at this stage and other officers attend to him, while I take a step back. An ambulance is called for and he comes-to pretty quickly, which we're all thankful for. You never ever go out on patrol wanting to hurt anyone, quite the opposite in fact: you go out on patrol to help people and catch the bad guys.

Anyway, he gets carted off to hospital in the back of an ambulance, along with a couple of officers, while I make my way back to the station to write up my notes about what happened.

Once he was at the hospital, his injuries were attended to by the staff there and he was kept in most of that night. It was only coming in to work later that next night duty I was told he had played up so much at the hospital and been so abusive to the nurses there that they had stapled his head injury back together at an odd angle, on purpose!

He probably looks like Harry Potter now.

He had also been arrested at the hospital and later that day charged with Criminal Damage and Threatening Behaviour I believe. His blood tests showed he had a high level of cocaine in him and that mixed with all the alcohol he had consumed was his undoing.

The icing on the cake was a handwritten letter from him to me, apologising for trying to attack me in the High Street!

31.

Fatal Accidents

Fatals are never a pleasant call to attend because, as the name implies, some poor soul has lost their life.

One I attended was a lad on a pizza delivery motorbike. It wasn't his; in fact it was stolen locally that very day. He had been flying through a crossroads without slowing down and ignoring the give way markings on the road and had clipped a car travelling normally, coming from his left. He had come off, skidded across the road, hit the kerb and came to a very sudden stop against a metal street light pole.

We had arrived on scene just seconds before the ambulance, who had been called by the driver of the car involved. The welfare of the rider was obviously the number one priority and, helping the ambulance crew, we all tried in vain to save the young lad's life. It quickly became apparent from the ambulance crew that the rider had probably died upon impact with the street light and there was little any of us there could do for him. His life was pronounced extinct by one of the paramedics at the scene and the wheels were set in motion for the arrival of specialist accident investigators to properly investigate the accident, identifying the deceased, finding and securing witnesses and the setting up of cordons so the scene could remain sterile, while trying to keep the regular flow of traffic moving. They are always a very busy and intense incident to deal with.

When it came time for the deceased to be taken away, I volunteered to go as what is called a 'continuity officer' in the back of the ambulance, which basically means there is a single officer who can link the scene, to the body, to any later identification at a mortuary. Saves it all getting a bit disjointed, with different officers doing different roles.

The next day I was required to attend the mortuary to identify the deceased, as of course I was the continuity officer. It really is just a case of turning up and confirming that the body laid out before you is one and the same as the body you had arrived with the day before. Trouble was this was my day off and I was looking after my son while my wife was at work. So he came along to the mortuary with me and stayed in the office part, playing with a few toy cars while I went and did the identification.

Although I had arrived at the correct time, a bit early in fact, the staff had already started work early on the post mortem. The young lad was laid out on one of the mortuary tables, with the top of his head missing and with his face completely peeled back from the skull. 'Is this the same male?' I was asked. 'I suppose so,' I said, 'but when I came in with him, he still had a face and head intact!'

On another occasion, early one morning, a guy had driven up a junction coming from a very busy dual carriageway and didn't even try to slow down when he got to the roundabout at the top. Trouble was this roundabout held a tube station in the middle of it and as a result there was a very large thick brick wall surrounding the centre of it and he had hit this at some considerable speed.

Upon our arrival, it was clear he had hit the wall at a high speed, the car was only about 3/4 its original length and the driver didn't appear to have been wearing a seatbelt. It looked like he had hit the windscreen too, but was sitting slumped unconscious in the driver's seat. He was the only occupant. We had requested for more units to join us and had also called for an ambulance and were told one had already been called.

I was posted with a good friend that day and we tried to prise the doors open to the car on both sides, but the impact had wedged them closed.

The driver appeared not to be breathing, so it was essential we started CPR as soon as possible. The impact may have given him neck or spinal injuries too, so we had the added problem of moving him. The answer to that is quite simple. We either left him there to die because he wasn't breathing, or risked moving him and possibly had the outside chance of worsening any injuries, but attempting CPR and saving a life. It was blatantly obvious – we needed to get him out.

We had the idea of smashing the back windscreen and dragging him out through there. In the cars we carried glass hammers, so I grabbed ours from our car and smashed the back windscreen, along with the rear passenger door windows on both sides.

This gave more access to the driver and my friend climbed in and using the car seat reclining handle, managed to get the driver's seat tipped as far backwards as it would go. We both clambered onto the boot and reaching through the newly smashed back window, we managed, with a lot of difficulty, to drag the large chap out through the window, assisted by some other officers who had arrived.

By this time the ambulance crew had arrived and they asked us to commence CPR on the man, which I did, just doing the chest compressions only as they requested.

Alas he didn't make it, being killed upon impact with the steering wheel and windscreen it would appear. And we never found out what had happened; whether it was done on purpose, or a terrible accident. As I say, you just go from job to job and often never get to hear about the final outcomes a lot of the time.

One of the worst that I ever dealt with, in regards to being a heartbreaking one, was a collision on a mini-roundabout between a large HGV (Heavy Goods Vehicle) and a minibus.

As I arrived on scene, the vehicles had collided in the centre of the roundabout and the cab of the lorry had struck the A pillar of the minibus. This had the double effect of bending it in towards the driver and also the opposite force of him being thrown up against it.

I opened the passenger door and quickly climbed inside onto the passenger seat. He had struck his head and was bleeding extremely heavily from his mouth. He was unresponsive to my speaking to him, didn't appear to be breathing, but hadn't gone completely limp, like there was still some life left in him. And right there and then as he sat in the driver's seat, I undid his seatbelt and started to do chest compressions on him while he was sitting upright. I really couldn't tell if he was breathing or not, such was the amount of blood gushing from the guy's mouth, so I just continued to do chest compressions on him, getting a lot of his blood over me, until someone else opened the driver's door. With this I stopped doing what I was doing, got out and ran over to the driver's side. I continued doing chest compressions on him and could sense his body was losing some of its rigidness and he appeared to go completely limp. I suppose you could say he died in my arms, that's certainly the impression I've always had of the incident. Quite a few other officers had arrived by this time, along with an ambulance crew and shortly after HEMS landed on scene too (the air ambulance).

One memory I have of this was of the lorry driver; he was still at the scene and was holding his hands up to his head, saying repeatedly, 'What have I done, what have I done?' My friend gave him a roadside breath test, which he failed. He hadn't been drinking that morning, but still had a skinful from a drinking session the night before in his system.

Some months later at Crown Court, where we all gave evidence, he was sentenced to four years in prison for 'Causing death by careless driving whilst under the influence of drink'.

Now the reason why I said this was heartbreaking, was the fact that I'd volunteered to do the death message to the family. I never saw his wife, only his sister. The reason I never saw the wife myself, was that she was still in the maternity ward at a local hospital.

He had been a new father for seven hours.

Just a little one here now as I've mentioned HEMS (Helicopter Emergency Medical Service), the Air Ambulance. It was not long after this fantastic service had first been formed that I had one turn up at an incident I was dealing with, along with a couple of other officers. It was the first time any of us had ever actually seen one of them. A poor lady had fallen through her loft hatch and had come crashing down with her legs either side of her bannisters on the first floor landing. Whatever you're imagining in your head right now is exactly what had happened to her. Enough said.

32.

What's the Time?

It's all getting a bit heavy now, so time for a bit of light relief.

Whilst working at the airport, I took a call to a male who had stolen a very expensive watch from a store display. Now being Heathrow Airport, nothing is cheap here; everything is top-end shopping and very expensive.

It was common practice for some passengers there, who didn't want to pay for what they wanted, to wait until the final boarding call for their flight, then commit the theft, and run to the gate just as the flight was closing, hoping they'd get away with it. And more often than not they did, as the cost of delaying a flight and upsetting the flight schedule was far more expensive than a watch, some sunglasses or a purse, so Heathrow often wouldn't delay a flight for us to board it and search for a suspect, with the outside chance they may not even be on that flight.

Anyway, this one time the description of the man who took the watch was that he was possibly Chinese in appearance. Now he could have got onto any flight, but a quick check of the flights shortly to leave revealed one was going to Beijing in China and it was going not from Terminal 5A where the theft had happened, but Terminal 5B and to get to this location was a good 10-minute journey.

I left the officers taking the report in 5A and drove over to 5B and walked around the gate where the flight to Beijing was leaving from.

As luck would have it I saw a guy exactly fitting the description of the suspect thief. I saw him take a seat by a window overlooking the airfield and walked up to him.

Now this is the part that if you watched it play out on a TV show you'd say how totally unbelievable it was, but I assure you this is exactly how it played out.

I stood in front of him and asked, 'Have you got the time mate?'

He pulled his sleeve up to reveal he was wearing two watches on the one wrist, before realising what he had done and whipped his sleeve back down fast!

'Gotcha pal, you're nicked!'

33.

Research Always Pays Off

Patrolling one night duty, a call came out to a nasty accident where one of the drivers involved had run away from the scene leaving the other driver badly injured. Not an unusual thing to happen, but straight away you're thinking about different scenarios; for example, whether the car is stolen, or if the driver has been drinking or on drugs. Many times people will run away from an accident of their making, make their way home and then ring the police to report their car has just been stolen. Happens a lot more than you'd think.

Anyway, a description had been given on the radio, of the driver who had run off, by other officers at the scene who were dealing with the actual accident. So, casting our net wide, I started to look for the suspect a bit further away from the scene of the accident, working out just how far he could have got if he was running.

After a short time and about a mile away from the scene of the accident, I saw a man waving down a taxi that was driving past him and, spinning the car around, I stopped it before it managed to drive off.

I got the man out and he fitted the description pretty well – age, build, jeans and a grey polo shirt. The man was also sweating and breathing heavily as if he'd been running. A quick name check on the Police National Computer and lo and behold, he had the same surname as the registered keeper of the car involved in the accident.

He failed a breath test and I arrested him for 'Drink drive', 'Failing to stop at the scene of an accident' and 'Suspicion of theft of the car'.

However, upon getting him back to the police station, once under the white strip lights of the custody suite, this grey polo shirt turned out to be bright orange with a blue collar. It couldn't have looked more different to the clothing description we'd been given over the radio.

He was left for the early turn CID to deal with and when I came in the next night, I discovered he had been charged with 'Drink drive', 'Failing to stop at the scene of an accident' and 'Aggravated vehicle taking', which is basically taking a car without the express knowledge or consent of the owner and causing damage or injury whilst driving it. It was quite a new offence back then.

I guessed he might plead guilty before any court date was set, but I ended up getting a court warning for him at the local Crown Court some months later.

I knew that the subject of his wildly different coloured top might come up as a sticking point with his defence, so I went down to the library near where I lived (yes, pre-internet days) as I was sure the top looked a different colour because of the old yellowish sodium style street lights.

I managed to find some information about them and swotted up until I knew it off by heart, so sure was I that the matter would come up as a part of his defence.

And indeed, come the day of the trial, I was stood in the box at Crown Court giving my evidence and being cross-examined and the defence brief holds up the shirt in all its bright orange glory and said, 'Officer, is this the 'grey' shirt you say my client was wearing on the night he was arrested?'

'Yes, indeed it was Your Honour,' I replied to the bench. 'Would you like me to explain the effects of sodium street lighting on the colour absorption of certain materials, especially at night?'

'No need officer,' came the reply, as he lowered the shirt, surprised at my reply - and that cut down that line of questioning straight away.

The final upshot of this though was that he was indeed the brother of the owner of the car. He had taken it while his brother had been away.

I didn't hang around for the final verdict; I never did with court cases. Once I'd given my evidence and was dismissed, I was out of there. I'd done my part. But as I was leaving during a break in the proceedings there, I saw the man I'd arrested by the exit door of the court. 'Sorry about all this,' he said to me, 'but I've got to give it a go, haven't I?'

I used to quite enjoy court. I used to go in with the attitude of 'I will not be beaten' and quite liked the cross-examination side of things, especially if you knew your stuff and had all the answers in your head to things you might be cross-examined on.

34.

PLAN

Carrying on with the court theme, I took a call that had come out to a domestic assault. Upon arriving, it turned out to be an Asian family, with multiple generations all living under the one roof. The husband and wife had been arguing and the wife's mother had decided to get involved. She had a few choice words to say to her son-in-law and he had ended up pushing her. Now, maybe due to the fact that the mother-in-law was as wide as she was tall (not very), she toppled over and had ended up breaking a hip on the hard floor.

I arrested the son for domestic assault, ABH (Actual Bodily Harm) but not before I had simply asked him, 'What's happened here mate?'

Now before I carry on, I'll just explain that some months prior to this, new rules and working practices had come in, based around the Human Rights Act. One of these was that all police actions must be Proportionate, Legal, Accountable and Necessary (PLAN).

Everything we did, from planning to arrests, everything, had to conform to this. This caused lots of moaning amongst officers, most seeing it as just more red tape and obstacles put in our way when we're just trying to keep the streets safe.

Now when this arrest and subsequent charge appeared before the courts, I was called to give evidence and questioned by the defence brief. They were going on about how and why I had asked 'What's happened here mate?' and how this was questioning the defendant before I had cautioned him and how anything he had said to me in reply should be struck from the court records as inadmissible evidence.

The defence turned to me and said, 'So why did you do it, officer?' thinking she now had one up on me.

I remember this so clearly, I turned to the bench (where the judges sit) and explained, 'What if the wife and her mother had some hidden agenda? What if they had some axe to grind with the defendant? Is it not proportionate, legal, accountable and oh so very necessary Your Honour, to simply ask 'What's happened here?'

They thought for a split second and replied 'Yes, it is officer, you're right'.

I'll never forget this; the defence brief looked down at her notes, as if studying them. She said nothing and the courtroom was silent.

It must have been silent for around 10 seconds, not long, but in that situation, it seemed an absolute age.

She raised her head in the end and said, 'No more questions' and sat down!

Most coppers working the streets go to court a lot during the course of their job. Not because the evidence is weak, but mostly because the defendant and their solicitors are planning on the police making some cock-up in the evidential process, thus getting the defendant off on some technicality. Some just want their day in court and to 'give it a run' in case they're found not guilty.

I was at court once and there was a WPC sitting in the police room waiting to give evidence, who was as nervous as hell. She had 22 years' service in the Royal Parks Police and this was the first time she had ever given evidence at court. It begs the question, had she been hiding under a rock all this time?

35.

Written in Blood

One last one on the subject of court. I was working an early shift and was summoned that very day whilst on duty, out of the blue, to the Royal Courts of Justice in The Strand. The judge sitting and presiding over a case had personally asked for me to attend and I thought, 'What trouble could I be in? What case was it to do with?

It stemmed from a job I did once where a woman had been sectioned under the Mental Health Act. We were assisting social services with the job and they were also taking her child into care, so serious were their concerns.

The flat where they lived was in a terrible state, the child massively neglected, living only on a dirty mattress on the floor, with no toys or suchlike. It made your heart bleed, especially if you were a parent yourself.

Once inside the flat, we saw that the mother had cut her wrists before we had arrived, not in any suicide attempt, just the actions of a crazy person to put it bluntly. She had written various unintelligible words over the internal walls of her flat in her own blood. There was mould everywhere and little food in the kitchen.

Once we had dealt with it and finished there, I did a form for our child welfare team, on a Form 74 if memory serves me correctly. I had written at the bottom of the form, in capital letters, with highlighted stars on either side for good measure, that under no circumstances should this child ever be returned to the parent. I even think I underlined it for good measure!

Now this case at the court was the mother trying to get her child back to live with her.

I arrived at the court for the afternoon session and stood in the box ready to give any evidence if required, or to otherwise account for my actions on the day.

I even remember the mother sat in the courtroom, giving out little snarls and groans.

However, I wasn't required to give any evidence of any kind. I wasn't even asked to justify the words I had written on this Form 74, a copy of which the court had.

The judge sitting had just requested me to attend to commend me personally on the words I had written on the form, saying that most officers would never have the guts (he might have used the word 'gumption') to write their personal feelings on such a form.

So I wasn't in any trouble; quite the opposite, I had a judge's commendation instead. Winner!

Did she get her child back – I have no idea. I hope not for the child's sake.

36.

One Unders

Not a phrase known to most, but the term 'one under' is the general term for a person who has committed suicide by throwing themselves under a train. One of the grounds I worked at had a railway station on it that had the highest number of 'one unders' of any station in the whole of the UK.

One of the reasons that helped it earn that horrendously unenviable title was when a mother clutching her two young children threw herself in front of a high-speed train. I wasn't on duty the day this happened, but I was on duty the day, exactly two weeks later, that the grandmother of the children, obviously in such mental anguish one couldn't imagine, threw herself in front of a train at the same station. It's an image you'll never forget, and I think of other passengers stood on the platform. What must they have seen and how has it affected them going forward? Do they have an image stuck in their minds they can't forget? Don't even get me started on the unfortunate train driver and their emotions.

I attended another 'one under' at this same station a couple of years later. It was a young girl, a schoolgirl, who had jumped in front of a high-speed train that was coming though. I remember her limbs scattered over the track and thinking how small and thin they were. What had been troubling her so much that she saw this as the only way out? 'What of her parents?' I often think. What was their reaction, who informed them, how could such a tragic event be avoided?

That's just it. In a way some of these awful suicides can't be avoided as such. All too often people don't like to expose their 'weaknesses' for want of a better word. They can keep it bottled up inside, seemingly fine on the outside, but inside all hope is gone and mentally they are broken and one day they snap and end their lives in ways such as this.

I was first on scene to another 'one under' at a different railway station and yet again a poor soul had leapt out in front of a high-speed train that was passing through the station. As I was walking down the platform, I casually kicked a piece of what I thought was a bit of stone or a broken ashtray out of my way but was in fact the top of the person's skull. It was strange; it appeared as clean as a piece of porcelain. Such was the speed of the impact that it had wiped away any trace of hair or tissue.

When these awful events occur, as much of what is left of the body is recovered as is humanly possible, but as you can imagine, there's a large amount of the body that is just completely destroyed and unrecoverable and scattered over a long distance in amongst the stone ballast under the tracks; there's no denying the fact. In most instances, the Fire Brigade are called and they hose the area down of things like body fluids, etc., hopefully leaving as little a trace as is possible.

I never got to know the reasons behind a lot of these suicides on the railways, as the investigation side of things is completed by the British Transport Police, a separate police force in its own right.

Maybe sometimes it's better not knowing.

37.

Getting Your Affairs in Order

I clearly recall the first ever time I gave CPR to someone. (Well, in the police anyway. I had given it to an old chap who had collapsed in a High Street once when I was a 16-year-old lad working at Sainsbury's. A passer-by was giving him mouth-to-mouth and instructed me to do the chest compressions, which I did until an ambulance turned up. I never found out what happened to him, I just carried on working at the shop and that was that.)

It was a call to a lady who had collapsed while out walking her dog on the large area of grass outside of her home. I even remember her full name to this day. As I arrived on scene, she was lying on the grass, still with her dog lead in her hand and the little dog just stood there.

It was clear she wasn't breathing and after making sure an ambulance had been called, I tilted her head back and, making sure her airway was clear and using a little clear plastic face shield, I commenced a mixture of mouth-to-mouth and chest compressions, stopping every now and then to check there had been no change in her condition. The ratio of breaths to chest compressions seems to be an ever-changing amount over the years, but back then it might have been two breaths to fifteen chest compressions, or something like that.

I was joined by a friend of mine who was responding to the call and together we shared the breaths and chest compressions until the ambulance turned up. CPR is surprisingly very tiring work, both mentally and physically.

The ambulance crew took over from us, and then they continued with the CPR as we followed them to the hospital. (I think a neighbour of the lady had taken care of the dog, in case you were wondering.) Speaking to the ambulance crew at hospital, they reckoned they had detected a weak pulse on the lady, but once in A & E, she had passed away. I'll never forget the exact words of the paramedic; 'We had just about kept her going, until they killed her in there!' No matter what your experience or profession, maybe we all make mistakes; it's just that some have much more serious consequences than others.

We had taken the lady's keys from her at the hospital and made our way back to where she lived. It's important for obvious reasons to try and trace next of kin and inform them of what has happened.

When we entered her house, she had a table set up in her hallway. On this propped up, was a sheet with all her details on, headed 'In The Event of my Death'. She must have known she wasn't long for this world and there written down neatly in order, were her full details, her next-of-kin, the name of her doctor, where to find her will and house deeds and what funeral arrangements she wanted, along with a few other bits and bobs.

Now that's planning for you.

38.

Defib Time Again

As I mentioned previously, as a police officer, doing CPR is not something you forget in a hurry. I've personally given CPR 13 times in my service, sometimes with a successful outcome, sometimes not. I've given it to elderly gents who have had a heart attack whilst clearing the ice from their cars early in the morning, to others who have overdosed on drugs and others of various ages who have collapsed either through a medical condition or suicide.

One that sticks out vividly happened towards the end of my service at Heathrow. I was patrolling with a good friend when we heard a really painful, tortured scream. The scream had come from literally 20 or 30 yards away from us and we ran over to where it had come from.

There was a middle-aged guy lying on the floor with a serious head injury from the impact with the stone tiled floor as he collapsed. He was bleeding profusely and because we were situated on a gentle incline, blood was running down the ramp.

There was another man standing above him, who was the guy who had let out the scream. He was the partner of the man who'd collapsed, as they were making their way towards their aircraft to start their holiday.

My friend and I both knelt down by the collapsed male as other airline staff were coming towards us, having also heard the scream. We had called for an ambulance and other officers were putting up on the radio that they were coming to our assistance also. Often you don't have to ask for assistance, on a tight close-knit team officers look out for one another and help is never very far away.

I had told airport staff to get cloths or whatever they could lay their hands on, in a bid to try and stem the profuse bleeding from the head injury.

It was while we were doing this that it became apparent the man was totally unresponsive. A quick check of his chest and mouth revealed that he was not breathing at all. One of the airline managers ran up to me and asked, 'What can I do?' I asked if he could get a defibrillator quickly and he ran off to find one. A staff member handed me a large roll of blue paper towel and as I started doing chest compressions on the man, my friend was getting large wads of the blue paper and trying to stem the severe bleeding from the head wound.

The mouth-to-mouth part of CPR isn't always required in the immediate aftermath of a collapse, especially one where you arrive so soon after it happens. There is an amount of oxygen already in the blood, so to start with it's just a case of doing good deep chest compressions to circulate that blood and keep vital oxygen moving around the body, especially to the brain.

It was while we were doing this and accidentally getting a good amount of blood on us (although we were both wearing the blue latex gloves at this stage that every officer keeps on themselves) that the partner of the collapsed male blurted out, 'He's HIV positive'.

Now I must confess here, that made little, in fact no difference to what we were doing. All that was going through our minds was to keep this guy alive.

The airline manager arrived back with a defibrillator and I ripped the guy's shirt open and attached the pads and I got the manager to turn the machine on. The leads were plugged in and I continued with the chest compressions. The defib analysed the patient and it advised a shock, which I delivered after making sure nobody was in contact with him physically, or they'd get the shock too. His body rose and tensed up and the machine told me to carry on with the chest compressions, which I did. It analysed the man again and the defib told us to shock him again, which we did.

At this stage, other officers arrived and while leaning over and delivering these chest compressions, a good friend of mine took away my MP5 carbine rifle I had stowed across by back when I had knelt down and undid my ballistic body armour and took it off me, so I was more free to do what I was doing. Another friend inserted an oropharyngeal airway into the man's mouth to help maintain an open airway. This is basically a rigid curved plastic tube that stops the tongue blocking the throat (which could stop his breathing). The defib analysed a third time and said to deliver yet another shock. This time as I shocked the man, his arms tensed up and after a couple of seconds, he let out a scream and tried to curl up into a ball. He was back with us. He had a very muscular build and it took some effort to control him as his body appeared to go into a spasm, bearing in mind we were still trying to control the head bleed too. His eyes remained closed and he had no control over his body's involuntary movements at all, as he seemingly fought against us.

Quite a few other officers had arrived and also the ambulance had turned up by this stage and a paramedic first responder for good measure too. The man was eventually transferred over to their care, alive and well. Well, certainly alive anyway.

The man's partner, when we were asking about the medical history of the patient, readily confessed that his partner had taken a lot of recreational drugs the night before and had been drinking a bit that morning and that he had just seemed to collapse with no warning at all as they walked to the gate to board their aircraft.

Despite all this effort, same as before, I never heard from either of them again. I've learnt never to expect thanks from anyone. We'd done our job and a pat on the back from friends and colleagues is recognition enough of a job well done.

Going on from this incident, due to a few of us getting the patient's blood on us, we were required to go along to

St Thomas' Hospital up by Westminster Bridge for the initial stages of HIV infection checks. I saw the nurse and she curtly asked me in her thick West African accent, 'Did you get any of the blood in your eyes?'

'Not sure,' I said. 'I got it on my face and nose'.

'Did you get any in your eyes?' she asked again, even more bluntly this time.

'I don't know,' I say, 'but I did get it on my face and nose, that's all I know'.

'You haven't got HIV,' she simply says, gets up and walks off.

'Cheers for that then,' I think. 'You've been a great help'. The wife wouldn't come near me for weeks after either, worried I was infected with HIV!

39.

Stop and Search

Now here's a subject I'm just going to deal with quickly, as views on this get very boring very quickly. It's a necessary requirement in the fight against crime, but as with most things, it must be done proportionately and only when needed. Believe me, the last thing in the world I want to do, or any police officer come to think of it, is to put our hands in someone else's pockets, not if I can help it, thank you very much.

One thing I'd always teach new officers when I was doing Street Duties Courses (remember, their first 10 weeks on the streets at their new station after completing their training at Hendon) was, whatever it is you're dealing with, is to EXPLAIN what you're doing and why you're doing it. It makes your job so much easier and at the end of the day, do you want to do a job the hard way, or the easy way for the same end result? If you explain exactly why you're doing what it is you're doing, people are much more understanding. You're still the police, you're in control of the situation and they're still the suspect, but come on, just don't be an ass about it.

One example, of a few I can think about of how this benefited me, was a young black lad I had arrested for possession of a knife which he had hidden up his sleeve.

He was dealt with firmly but fairly and I think he received a caution for possession of an offensive weapon. A few weeks later, as I'm walking on my own late one evening going back to my car to go home after a late shift, I walk past a group of four or five lads and one of them is the lad who I'd arrested. He sees me and goes, 'Mr Officer, it's me you arrested with the knife'. He turns to his mates and says how I'm one of the good guys and goes to give me a fist bump, which I return. I ask if he's keeping out of trouble and we all have a little laugh and I go on my way. It could have had a different outcome.

It doesn't pay to 'wind up' prisoners, just deal with them firmly and fairly as I say. Always think of the officer who's got to deal with them after you.

Not a stop and search but another man I nicked for possession of an offensive weapon was the result of a call to police, about someone following commuters from a tube train late one evening. He had two large similar kitchen knives, one up each sleeve, with holes drilled in the handles and attached together with string that went up each sleeve and around the back of his neck. So all he had to do was shake his arms and he had a knife in each hand! Frightening stuff.

40.

Amazing World-First Lifesaving Work

I was doing a plain clothes operation with a good friend when through the radio earpiece we were wearing, we heard a call come out to a male who had jumped from the top floor of a multi-story car park. The car park in question was about 100 yards from our location, so we ditched the work we were doing and ran towards it. As I turned a corner, I saw a man lying in the road, looking very crumpled, lying in the nearside lane. It never ceases to amaze me, traffic was still driving by in the outside lane, driving around him, with not one car stopping to help. As we ran over to him, I gave the exact location out on the radio and requested an ambulance and other officers to come and assist.

He was facing up, with his eyes wide open, but was totally unresponsive to any speech. His legs looked shattered and he had open fractures – bones sticking out of his lower limbs and was bleeding heavily from these injuries. We knelt down by his side and quickly saw that he was breathing, so the first thing was to try and somehow stem this heavy blood loss before he bled to death right there on the roadside. Lying down alongside his legs, I tried to jam my elbow into his femoral artery, hoping that the narrowing of this might help slow the bleeding. My friend was doing the same on the other side, bearing in mind we had run there and didn't have any kind of first aid kit with us. The first police vehicle that turned up gave us their first aid kit and then repositioned their car to afford us some protection, as I clearly remember traffic driving past us literally just a foot away from where my legs were lying.

It was raining slightly and his blood ran out and mixed with the water on the wet road, so it seeped into my trousers and my jacket. Not an issue at the time, his need was far greater than mine.

We managed to get some thick wound dressings out of the first aid kit and now there were three of us working on him, we could apply some pressure around all of his open fractures too. I remember one officer who turned up, who was actually a first aid instructor. He had called out to put the man in the recovery position. 'No,' we called out, as if that had been done we wouldn't have been able to control the bleeding, which was the primary concern at that stage. The man was breathing anyway, albeit quite shallow, we'd just have to closely monitor that. I asked that officer to go up to the top of the car park and search for any car, or a suicide note, etc.

One of our ARV's (Armed Response Vehicles) arrived, who carried more of a comprehensive first aid kit and between us all we were making a decent job of reducing his blood loss. He was still at this stage completely unresponsive to any speech, or to any pain we might have caused as we were applying direct pressure to his wounds, although his eyes were still very wide open.

A locally based paramedic turned up and upon seeing what we were doing, just told us to carry on and suggested little tweaks here and there to best improve his chances. I said to search the man's pockets while we were doing all this, to try and find a wallet and hopefully a name, an address, etc. One of the sergeants present who was standing by us said, 'You can't do that!' I mean, what planet was he on? Of course we could, it's called trying to trace next of kin, identifying the poor bloke and letting his family know what's happened.

Splints were applied to parts of his legs, just to try and make them a bit more secure and before we knew it (believe me time absolutely flies by when you're doing this) HEMS, the Air Ambulance, arrived.

It had started to rain a bit heavier now and upon the doctor assessing the casualty, there was a bit of a discussion amongst the medical team and a plan of action was decided by them. The pilot came over from the helicopter with a large sheet and he placed it over us as we still worked on the man. Now this is where it all got a bit surreal.

There were now four of us under the sheet, three police officers and the doctor. Five including the casualty.

The doctor asked us if we were OK to assist him and we all agreed obviously. The doctor asked me to hold his mobile phone up towards him, which I did, as he handed various packaged sterile medical implements to my colleagues. I could see on his phone screen that he was talking to what was another doctor, who appeared to be at home sitting in his kitchen.

Now without getting too technical, which is impossible anyway as this was way beyond anything I'd ever seen before, he started to perform a procedure called a REBOA, which stands for Resuscitative Endovascular Balloon Occlusion of the Aorta (got to thank Google for that one).

It's a medical procedure to help control severe pelvic haemorrhage, where a balloon is fed into the bottom end of the aorta, the largest blood vessel in the body and then inflated, cutting off the blood supply to the damaged blood vessels in the lower part of the body.

I knelt there holding his phone while the doctor on the other end talked it through with the doctor under the cover with us. My two colleagues unpacked and handed him the tools he was using as and when he asked for them.

Once stable, the patient was transferred to the helicopter and it took off to a Central London hospital.

The officer who had gone up to the top floor of the car park did indeed find a suicide note there and the man's car. It was months later I found out that a lot of this incident had been filmed by a taxi driver parked in the multi-storey car park opposite and he had posted it on YouTube.

The jumper did actually survive his fall and the last I heard about him, he was wheelchair bound. I hope he's recovered further.

The incident and subsequent REBOA procedure made headline news actually, on the BBC, Sky News and quite a few others. Apparently it was the first time in history the pioneering procedure had been used outside of a hospital setting anywhere in the world. Even the London Mayor had made comments about it on television.

And just to cap it all off, we all got a formal complaint made against us by the man's parents, which basically said we didn't do anything right, he must have been pushed, he'd never have jumped and how the whole way we had dealt with it was botched. The complaint wasn't successful; it didn't go anywhere of course.

You just can't win sometimes. And they wonder why police morale is low!

41.

ATM Robbers

It was 1am and a very good friend of mine and a superb copper said, 'God, I wish something would happen, I'm bored'.

Be careful what you wish for.

Literally about five seconds later, a call came out over the radio to an armed robbery in progress right then, at a very big local hotel, with staff saying a vehicle had driven into the hotel foyer, by smashing through the entrance doors and coming to a rest in the lobby area. They said that explosives had been used to blow an ATM machine from the hotel foyer wall and that they, the staff, had been threatened with what they thought was a firearm. The vehicle, a black BMW X5 had driven off with the ATM machine in the back of it.

Now just by coincidence, as this came out over the radio, two other friends of mine from my team saw the same X5 drive past right in front of them, with the ATM machine still sticking out the back of it and they started to give chase.

Another coincidence (who'd have believed it, eh?), the force helicopter from our Air Support Unit, call sign India 99, was just about directly overhead, as it was conducting security patrols of the very same area.

As they followed the X5, unknown to them, there was a second bandit vehicle involved, travelling in convoy with the X5 (any vehicle you chase involved in the crime is the 'bandit' vehicle; it has been known as this since I joined the job); this other vehicle being a very powerful Audi RS6. My two mates were rammed during the initial stage of this pursuit by this Audi, putting the officers and their vehicle out of action, and my mates sustaining only minor injuries thankfully.

An Armed Response Vehicle (ARV) had been closing in on the chase too and had driven towards the X5. They had collided and the X5 with the ATM in the back had landed up in a ditch. A small foot chase in the dark ensued, but the X5 occupants had managed to get into the accompanying Audi and flee the scene, pursued by the helicopter and another police vehicle.

The Audi proved too fast and powerful to be followed by the police car, but they couldn't outrun the helicopter, which gave a running commentary on its location at all times.

The Audi passed through a few local towns that I knew and I recognised that it appeared to be doubling back on itself. A few of us started to make our way to the general area we thought it might be heading to and we were correct, as the Audi had ended up driving into a small residential road where the occupants were seen to be ditching either clothing or tools involved in the crime. And unknown to the robbers, officers were now very close behind them.

Another of our ARVs had entered the close with a view to making arrests at gunpoint, but upon seeing them the Audi repeatedly rammed their car, putting both vehicles out of action. The suspects, I believe four of them, climbed over fences and low roofs and tried to run away. As they were doing this, the helicopter was still giving a running commentary on their locations, with one of the suspects hiding in the grounds of a church. I knew where this church was, having grown up only a couple of miles away.

As I drove up to the church, I leapt out of the car, grabbed my MP5 (the carbine rifle remember), made sure the glowing dot of the Eotech was on, flicked the selector (safety catch) to the off position and began a search for the suspect. By pressing the front foregrip of the weapon, it activates the built-in torch under the muzzle and listening to the directions being relayed by the helicopter observer overhead, I closed in on the suspect. I shouted, 'Armed police – show me your hands!' at the suspect who was crouched in a bush, but he leapt to his feet and was on his toes again. The selector was switched back to safe and a foot chase started, going over some nasty spiked fences in the dark – that's why the safety catch is put back on, it's just good drills.

Other firearm officers arrived and after a long foot chase, they went to ground (hid) and a containment was put in over quite a large area. Two suspects were arrested, one of them detained by two of my colleagues who were unarmed at that time and in the ensuing rough and tumble of a suspect not wanting to come quietly, I think he suffered a couple of cracked ribs where he fell during the struggle to escape, with the officers on top of him.

The other two had escaped on that occasion, but after that the rest of the investigation was down to the Flying Squad (yes, The Sweeney for those of a certain vintage).

I think they pleaded guilty at court as none of us were required at a trial and they received custodial sentences of several years. No firearms were found and the 'explosives' used to blow the ATM were some kind of compressed gas that was ignited, something that's been quite common up and down the land. The ATM was recovered, along with the X5 in the ditch.

All in all, a good night's work. Very late off work, home for a few hours' kip, then up and back in for the next night shift, hopefully for more of the same!

42.

Desire to be Shot

A call came out on the radio very late one winter's evening to an ex-partner making threats to kill a young lady informant and that he, the ex-partner, was currently parked up in her office car park.

Now the fact that he was actually on scene with the lady and she had used the words, 'threatening to kill me', it produced quite a comprehensive police response, with quite a few officers accepting the call and making their way to the scene.

(Just for the record here, you often get people bemoaning the police response to calls and there's the old joke about, 'I said I'd shoot him; that got them all here'. Yes, it would get the police there quicker, but that just means the people they were en route to see, other victims of crime – burglaries, thefts, domestics, missing people, etc., now just have to wait even longer to see an officer.)

It was whilst en route to the call, that the informant told us she thought he had been taking drugs and that he had talked about getting himself killed too. She had told the 999 call handler that her ex's brother had been shot by police some time in the past and that he had talked about wanting to 'go out the same way'. This put a whole new spin on things, as there was now no telling what his intentions were, or how he might react upon seeing police turn up.

The informant also told us he was in a black Volkswagen Golf and was still outside her office sat in the car. He had apparently already deliberately driven into some cars parked in the car park there.

As some of us arrived on the scene, we saw that the office was situated in a low-lying block of similar units, in a large courtyard-style setting, with two large vehicle entrance/exits. These exited out to a small service road and then out onto the main road. The suspect was sitting in his car as she had said, revving the engine hard. Rather than drive straight up to him, we parked by one of the entrances and got out. Any attempt to communicate with him just saw him rev his engine harder and then, out of the blue, he accelerated hard and braked and skidded just short of where my car was parked. He reversed and did this a second time.

Now knowing he was possibly on drugs as the informant had suggested, it was important to not let him get out and drive his vehicle on the public roads, as who knows what carnage he could have caused. As other officers arrived, they were instructed to block both entrances with their vehicles, giving him no chance to escape and cause harm to anyone. It had become a stand-off, with him driving around the courtyard, occasionally accelerating towards the police vehicles but braking at the last minute. The driver's window was down, but he made absolutely no attempt to engage in conversation with any of us.

We also received information from our control room that the suspect's car had come to the notice of police three separate times in the two hours leading up to the start of this incident: once for ramming another car on the road, for colliding with a motorcyclist and knocking him off, and for hitting some road signs, failing to stop in all these cases.

This state of affairs continued for some time and a dog unit, a dedicated traffic unit and a Trojan unit were requested (Trojan is the call sign of the London based ARV units), just because you want to prepare for all eventualities, after all we had no idea what he might have had with him in regards to weapons in his car.

Time was getting on, but there was no immediate rush. He was sitting in his car, he couldn't escape, the informant was still in her office where she had locked the door and if he had got out of his car, the distance between us meant he couldn't have got to her before we took him down.

The incident had come to the attention of other officers on neighbouring boroughs too and a van unit arrived on scene from a different police station just to lend a hand if needed. All help was gratefully received.

Upon the arrival of the ARV unit, all the info we had up to that point was explained to them. Speaking to one of the ARV officers (we later became good friends when we were on the same team together), he said to tell all the officers present not to use any CS spray on the suspect, just in case they were required to deploy a Taser on him. They explained there was a distant chance that the Taser could ignite the CS. At that point they didn't have any intention to deploy, but would remain parked very close by, in case the situation escalated.

Now the Taser is an invaluable tool. It can help end a violent individual's behaviour very quickly just by being present at the scene. I've deployed it on five or six occasions and just by 'lighting someone up' with the red sight dot, it can bring a volatile situation to a swift end; that is better for all concerned. Many suspects know you're not going to deploy a firearm against them; after all, this isn't America. But a Taser is a different matter altogether.

I told every officer individually the request from the Trojan unit re: the CS and everyone understood. The suspect every now and then would slowly drive around the courtyard and drive fast up to the line of police cars and then stop. He would also make 'gun' gestures with his hands at us, every now and then bang his head hard on his steering wheel, as well as pointing to an object in his car, of which we had no hope of seeing what it was. Every now and then he'd reach into his car and throw something at us, anything he could get his hands on really.

This pattern of behaviour suddenly started to increase, with the suspect repeatedly driving up fast and braking and skidding at the last moment, until he accelerated and rammed one of the police cars. He reversed and did this again and again, smashing up three vehicles, including the front of his own.

Once he had done this on one of the entrances, he turned his attention to the other. He wheel spun around in the courtyard and drove at speed into my vehicle. As he came to a halt for a second, one of the younger officers on scene there sprayed a jet of CS spray at the driver, in through his open window. 'No!' another officer yelled at him (by the way, this officer who deployed the CS was dismissed from the force about a year later for other matters).

Anyway, the suspect reversed hard and drove forward again, his engine revving loudly and smashed into the cars again. On the third time of doing this his engine suddenly died when he collided with the police cars. Some of us leapt over the remains of our vehicles and went forward to detain the suspect. I ripped open the driver's door, to be met with a flurry of punches from the driver. I had my baton drawn and struck him twice in the face with it, that being the only area of his body I could get at, as my left hand was trying to keep his arms down. In the close confines of the front seat of the car, he grabbed hold of my baton and as I tried to pull it from his grasp, the corded handle snapped and he was now holding my baton! As I fought with him, he struck me with it twice on the arm, not getting a good swing due to us being so close to one another. As I took a step back, bizarrely, he was hit with a blast of powder from a fire extinguisher, aimed by the officer who had arrived from a different station. Maybe he thought it a good distraction technique!

At this point the ARV officers had drawn their Tasers and were shouting orders at him to stop what he was doing. He didn't and was shot with a Taser fired through the now open passenger door. It seemed to have little effect, so he was shot with a Taser by another officer through the driver's door. It too had little effect, possibly due to the clothing he was wearing at the time, who knows? At this stage, he quickly got out of the car just as a good friend (who had climbed on top of the car) leapt off the roof of the suspect's car right onto him. Even though they collapsed onto the floor, the suspect stood up and, holding my baton, took a swing at the dog handler and his dog, who had now joined the violent fight. He tried to strike one of the ARV officers too, who was reloading his Taser. The ARV officer ran off into the courtyard followed by the suspect holding the baton above his head, followed by us. Just as the ARV officer had reloaded whilst running, he stopped, spun around, took aim and fired his Taser at the suspect, almost at point blank range. The barbs made good contact, one in the face, the other in the neck and he dropped to the ground, with all of us grabbing hold of a limb each and pinning him down. He was handcuffed and arrested for a variety of offences by one of the officers present.

Now all this sounds like it took quite a while from his car giving out to him being arrested, but in reality, it was probably no more than 10 to 15 seconds at the most. There was just so much happening, it takes a while to explain everything.

So, he didn't get his wish that night to be shot by police, but he was remanded in custody and received a spell in prison for his efforts.

It was a year or so after this event, that I sadly left this particular police station for another posting. One of the items I was presented with upon my leaving was my baton, which had originally been seized as evidence, beautifully set up in a large glass display case, with a brass plaque inscribed with the words 'the one that got away!'

43.

Everything but the Kitchen Sink

It's not uncommon to deal with a variety of violent people; some are violent just because they're part of the scum criminal element in society and some because of mental health issues.

A couple of officers who were assisting a mental health team from the local council in sectioning a chap under the Mental Health Act, had asked for some assistance as the man involved was 'playing up' and making threats towards them all. A couple of us who were shield trained (as in Public Order, such as disturbances and riots, etc.) offered to help and upon our turning up saw that the 'patient' had gone upstairs in the small terraced house and was throwing objects down at whoever got too close.

Now, this individual may not have been responsible for his own actions, hence he was to be sectioned, but he still needed to be detained and medically cared for.

Getting a pair of long shields from the van for protection from anything he might throw at us, we both entered the house and locking our shields together, went to move up the stairs, with the other two officers a short distance behind us. A couple of other officers had arrived too and were positioned just outside by the front gate, should anything untoward happen.

All of a sudden we started to have objects rain down upon us, first it was books and a couple of table lamps, but this was followed shortly after by the drawers from a bedside unit, all their contents, chairs, a small table, a mattress, bedding, the bed, then the actual bedside units themselves and the doors of a wardrobe. He also smashed up the bannisters by kicking them apart and was throwing them at us too. The stairwell was filling up quicker than we could empty it. Whatever was upstairs and not pinned down came our way.

As we managed to climb up and over some of this stuff and make our way to the top of the stairs, the man raced into a bedroom and flung himself Superman-style out of an open first floor window.

He came to rest in all the bushes in the garden, where he was detained and dealt with for, thankfully, (and amazingly) only minor injuries to himself. He was subsequently detained under the Mental Health Act and got the help he needed. I hope.

Events like these are all too common. I had to effect an entry once into the house of a serving police officer after his wife had suffered some sort of mental health issue and was literally smashing the house up with a baseball bat. Literally, a baseball bat. She was detained and received medical help due to her suffering some sort of nervous breakdown, which I've seen happen to people before.

Another was to a 16-year-old lad who was about 6'4" tall and when we entered his house (called by the parents), he was holding a chair above his head and screaming at the top of his voice. This one didn't go according to plan, as the team Inspector who was there with us deployed CS spray, but instead of hitting the lad with it, sprayed it onto our long shields, causing it to splash back into our faces. After we had semi-recovered, we continued with the entry and, still with eyes and noses streaming heavily, we managed to pin him down in the bathroom, secure him and detain him under the Mental Health Act.

I remember one lady with no history of mental illness, who was suffering a nervous breakdown, was just curled up in a ball under her table, just screaming and screaming. What was going on in her poor tortured mind I have no idea, but these people need treating with a great deal of compassion. After all, it's not their fault; they're not acting how they would normally and that's always got to be in the forefront of your mind when called to deal with them.

Some people need help, not punishment.

44.

Armed Robbery With a Sting in the Tail

The Friday night call we've all been longing for comes out from a frightened security guard, who's on the phone after ringing 999. He's saying that there's a robbery going on right now and that he'd been threatened with a knife and a baseball bat and also a firearm, but he hadn't actually seen the gun.

Now I say, 'waiting for', not meant in a flippant or glib way; it's just that as a street copper these types of calls are the reason you joined the job, a chance to take down serious criminals in the act. It's what the job's about.

The address he's given on the phone is one I'm familiar with. After working a ground for years, you get to know places, the geography of an area, the rat runs and the back alleys. As we near the location, I can see other blue lights heading our way and several of us descend on the building concerned at the same time. As we get out, I can see people running out the back of the building but can't get to them due to a very high spiked metal security fence. I knew that behind the building was a car parking area and there was easy access from the building next door. As some officers run into the building, I shout, 'Follow me' and a few of us run around to the back. As we get there, we detain one of the robbers straight away and after what is quite a violent struggle to subdue this first one, he's instantly handcuffed. As I'm doing this, I can see a friend of mine, a former Royal Marine Commando, repeatedly striking the knees of one of the suspects with his baton as they try to detain him while he's throwing punches at them. He's arrested too after a violent struggle, as is one other found still inside the building.

Every single one arrested puts up a violent fight in an effort to escape.

There's still one suspect though, who's seen by other officers jumping into a river that ran behind the buildings, to evade capture. Now this river at the time was very swollen and flowing fast and the last that was seen of him was him being carried away by the strong current, shouting for help.

Those of us who had made arrests for robbery, etc. were rather focused on what we were doing and carried on with the job in hand. It was a dog handler who had arrived who saw this suspect being swept away. One thing that struck me was whilst in custody, the suspect who had his knees repeatedly struck by my ex-Commando friend, showed not the slightest bit of pain. Probably the drugs taken before they started their robbery.

It was only a short time later that a senior officer decided to treat the missing suspect as a death in custody, because as far as anybody knew, he hadn't managed to get himself out of the river. Now this isn't a pleasant experience and it wasn't the first time I had been subject to an investigation into a death in police custody. Everything I was wearing was seized as evidence: body armour, shirt, trousers, boots, etc., and every bit of kit was similarly seized, from handcuffs to my baton.

No individual was ever reported as a 'missing person', no body was ever found, and it was assumed that he had managed to get himself out of the river after all. This was all decided some months later; mind you, it's not a speedy process and leaves a nasty taste in the mouth.

Now, I said it's not the first time I'd been investigated for a death in custody. The first time was as a result of a call to a domestic disturbance, where I'd arrested the male concerned. He had had a fight with his wife, (they were both in their late 60s I think) after a bit of a drinking binge and she had gone and locked herself in the bathroom. He had taken a huge knife from their kitchen and had started hacking away at the bathroom door to get at her, very 'Here's Johnny'…

When we arrived, he still had a hold of the knife, but showed us no aggression at all and he came quietly.

I'd arrested him for a domestic assault of some kind and after booking him in to custody, I placed him in one of the cells to sober up. I made sure he was settled and OK and went away to do my notes of the arrest.

There was no CCTV in the cells back then; it was a case of the Custody Officer or the Gaoler doing regular checks on the welfare of those detained.

Later that same night, I was called back to the station. The man had been found unresponsive in the cell, an ambulance had been called, but there was nothing they could do; he had unfortunately died in there.

We went through the due processes of a death in custody, having everything seized as evidence for the investigation, but not suspension from duty, which I thought strange.

The upshot of it all was that he was found to have had a heart attack in the cell and at the subsequent inquest the coroner stated it was probably brought on by his drinking, an apparently unknown heart condition he suffered from, and the stress of the fight with his wife. I had nothing to answer for, a result I was very grateful to receive.

At a Coroner's Court, you can be cross-examined, questioned if you like, by anyone there and I was questioned by the man's family. I'll never forget that they showed no anger towards me, absolutely no hostility at all. Maybe it's because I'd shown a great deal of remorse and pity at what had happened and a great deal of compassion for the wife and family. Who knows? It's an experience and another thread of life's rich tapestry as they say.

45.

Always Expect the Expected

In a working men's club in West London one evening, members of the Traveller Community were out celebrating a wedding. We had received prior warning of this and were informed of it at the start of our shift. The reason for the advanced warning was that there was a good chance of a fight breaking out, which is inevitably a large one, and towards the end of the night one almighty fight certainly did break out. It had ended up with a man receiving quite severe injuries, having been battered around the head until he was unconscious by a large fire extinguisher.

Another man had been arrested for the assault by other officers and the fire extinguisher had been seized by them as evidence. I was posted with a friend that night in the area car, and we offered to bring the fire extinguisher to the police station, as it was obviously evidence in the investigation of the assault. I put it in the back of our car and once all the disorder had calmed down to a degree, we left the scene to drive the mile or so back to the station.

Now, unknown to us, the safety pin and the tamper seal had been dislodged during its use as a club and once we had arrived back at the station, we had to drive up the slight ramp to get us into the rear yard.

As we did so, the foam fire extinguisher rolled onto its side, causing the handle to be squeezed under its own weight. Then all hell broke loose, I don't know if you've ever seen the force behind one of these things going off, but the noise and speed with which the foam comes out is nothing short of explosive!

In seconds we were both completely covered with white foam, as was the inside roof of the car, the windscreen, dashboard, just about every single surface. It looked like we were at an Ibiza foam party!

Officers came out of the station, with everyone grabbing their phones and taking photographs of us – it was like being pounced on by the paparazzi. As for the potential evidence obtained from the seized fire extinguisher, it was never needed, as no allegations were ever made by the lad who had been knocked out (it's just not their way. I'm sure a bit of summary justice was handed out some time later between the families concerned).

This leads me on to another minor incident where we were dealing with a group from the Traveller Community. I'm not too sure why we were dealing with them; it was a bit of disorder somewhere I think. Anyway, this lad gave me his name and date of birth and I did a name check on him on the Police National Computer and it came back as 'no trace PNC'. I had doubted from the off that he'd ever give his real name in a month of Sundays, so just to stir it up a bit, I went back to him and told him that he was wanted on the PNC and he'd have to come with me. He blurted out that he had given me a false name, gave me his real name and he was wanted for failing to appear at court, so was arrested anyway! So funny!

46.

Burglars

Now every copper worth his salt wants to nick burglars, burglary is a disgusting crime that never gets the punishment it deserves. It can leave people scared to be in their own home and I've even witnessed an elderly victim of a burglary have a heart attack and pass away days after being burgled, such is the stress it can cause some people.

I've stated previously that I'd often heard it said before I joined the job that you might come across a burglar in the act of thieving once in your service, and that my best was personally nicking six over a six-week period.

The first two were arrested together by myself, after ransacking a home just yards from a train station. They had come down on a train from a bit further into Central London, got off at this station and burgled a house in the road just behind it, and had run back to the station to get the train back from where they'd come from. A neighbour had heard smashing glass and called the police. The station seemed an obvious choice to head to first to search for them and there they both were on the platform, with a pillow case taken from the house (used as a bag to transport their stolen gear away, done far more often than you'd think). Inside the pillow case was the kid's electronic toys, cash, a laptop and the contents of the jewellery box owned by the lady of the house. They came quietly, luckily. I didn't really want to have a roll-around by railway tracks.

The next was a single lad who had smashed his way into a house, gone straight to the bedrooms and stolen all the jewellery he could find. Upon stopping him, also at a (different) train station as it happens, he had all the jewellery hidden in the turned-up part of his beanie hat and hidden in the turn-ups of his jeans. 'You're nicked son.'

The next ones arrested were also from a house burglary, where again someone had called the police because they saw them jump over a rear fence into a back garden. When we arrived they were still trying to get the big television out of too small a window frame and after a chase over gardens two were arrested by myself whilst trying to hide, along with another still in the house arrested by a colleague. It was quite strange to have three lads out burgling a house; it's normally just one or two maximum.

The last one arrested by myself was to a similar call, where I ended up chasing a guy over a garage roof, before grabbing him in a neighbour's back garden and arresting him.

There ended the busiest spell I'd ever had of arresting burglars caught in the act. Sure there have been plenty more, before and since, but never have I arrested so many in such a short space of time.

When you're investigating burglaries after they've happened, it never ceases to amaze me when neighbours say how they'd heard smashing glass, but never thought to look, or even to dial 999.

Often when you're called to a 'suspects on', meaning there's a burglary happening right there and then, you get a good police response – as I say, we all want to nick burglars; they're a filthy disease on society. What I've often done in the past, when we think the burglar is in back gardens somewhere, is to put in a containment. That is; having officers on all sides of the surrounding roads where you think the suspect is hiding up, and try and flush them out using a dog unit or just other officers. This is all well and good in London where sometimes you have the officer numbers and resources to do this, but in more rural areas of the country you might struggle for this kind of response.

Many's the time I've knocked on someone's house and explained the situation and asked to go up to their back bedroom to give me a view out across all the gardens and hopefully be able to direct any officers to any movement or suchlike.

I've never had anyone say no to that request, ever. In fact, they've been quite excited to be involved and I'm always extremely grateful to them afterwards.

47.

It's Not All About Arresting People

I had a call once to a shop situated in Heathrow Airport where the staff had stopped a lady of around 30 years of age for shoplifting. When I arrived, she was quite compliant and the staff explained to me they had stopped her for stealing two bottles of water. What? Who steals bottles of water?

It transpired upon talking to her, how she was essentially homeless and had been living at the airport for a few days (it happens every now and then; it's a warm safe environment for them). She was hungry and thirsty and had taken the water to drink. It's not like she was out stealing designer handbags or anything. The staff at the shop were keen to have her arrested, but there was no way on earth I was arresting a woman, or anyone for that matter, for stealing water just to try and survive and I told them so.

She explained to me how her church group that she belonged to were arranging somewhere for her to stay, but she had to get to them in the first instance – and that was the problem, no money for any sort of ticket out of there.

There was a charity actually based at the airport and a large part of their work was assisting stranded travellers. I took her there, explained the situation and they gave her a travel ticket enabling her to leave the airport, so she'd be no problem to anyone else in the future, as well as just giving someone a helping hand.

Not much of a story, but it does show the police do have a human, caring side; it's not always rushing around arresting people. It's a balancing act sometimes, between what the victim wants versus what the right thing to do is. Surely doing the right thing wins every time?

Shoplifters are part and parcel of everyday policing and can be a pain to deal with, as they take up a lot of time for very little result at the end of the day. I know it's still theft, but it's pretty low-level stuff. Some are more interesting than others though; for example, a favourite of East Europeans was the metal foil-lined bag trick where they'd steal clothing with security tags on and place them in a foil-lined bag so they wouldn't set off the alarm panels at the shop exits.

Similarly, if they didn't have foil-lined bags, they'd still steal the tagged clothing but while in the store they'd slip an item of tagged clothing into an innocent shopper's bags. When they walked out, they, the innocent party, activated the alarms and while security dealt with them and with the alarms still going off, the thief made their way out with their stolen items undetected.

Another would be women, often from the Middle East, wearing traditional dirty-looking long robed dresses, who'd have 'shoplifting pockets' sewn into their garments. The clothing was so multilayered, you couldn't even tell when they had multiple joints of meat hidden away in them, and more often than not they'd have young kids with them too, a nightmare to deal with!

Though I must admit, not so much a nightmare to deal with as someone in a wheelchair. Have a think about having to arrest someone in a wheelchair and how bad that could look to a passer-by? There was an old guy who used to live on the first ground I policed and he was known for keeping a golf club in the back of his wheelchair that he used to swing at people who he didn't like! One day he was trundling along the High Street, when he came across a BMW parked partly across the dropped kerb. He was known to be a very angry fellow and he proved it that day. He took his golf club from the back of his wheelchair and proceeded to smash the windows of the BMW and also strike at every body panel and light that he could reach! It was one of those arrests where you get into the custody suite and start by saying, 'Well, it's like this Sarge'…

Honestly, you couldn't make it up sometimes!

48.

Fleeing the Country

Not so long ago I took a call to one of the gate rooms at Heathrow where the additional security agents there, employed by this certain airline, had done a check on a passenger about to board and discovered that he was in possession of a forged passport.

(A forgery is a genuine document that has been altered in some way, like a different photograph placed in there or something like that. A counterfeit is when the entire document is made up or copied.)

As a colleague and I approached the gate room we were met a short distance from it by one of the security team. He handed me the forged passport and explained that when they had pointed out to the passenger that the passport was a forgery, he had collapsed onto the floor. They were sure this was some sort of distraction technique and that he was pretending as they said it all looked far too staged and controlled a fall, but for what end who knows? He had picked himself up pretty quickly when they had told him they knew he was only pretending and to get up off the floor and stop acting the fool.

I walked up to the man concerned, explained why we were there and asked his name. He refused to give it and in fact wouldn't answer any questions at all. I guessed he was fleeing the country because of some crime he'd committed, but he wouldn't give the game away or say anything.

We used to arrest a lot of people there who were trying to escape justice of one form or another. I've arrested everyone from armed robbers and rapists to a guy who was wanted for shooting someone in the face.

This man we were with could well have been trying to flee from something similar, but he just wouldn't tell us.

I arrested him for possession of a forged passport, to which he still made no reply and I knew we had quite a long walk back to where our van was parked. With this in mind, I turned to him and told him that I knew he'd faked fainting and collapsing onto the floor and I told him that if he pulled the same stunt with me, I'd drag him by his collar all the way out to the van. I'll never forget the look of shock on my colleague's face when I told the suspect this! Once he was handcuffed, he walked calmly out to the van where I sat him down in the rear cage. I wouldn't have dragged him all the way out by the scruff of his neck of course; it was really just to show we were taking no shit from him and we were not there to mess around in any way. And it obviously worked anyway.

I asked him his name one more time and this time he spoke. He said, 'I'll leave that to you to try and find out'. I told him it'd be pretty easy; we'd just put him on the fingerprint machine once in custody and if he was known to us we'd get his name pretty quickly. He thought for a moment. I asked him again and with a deep sigh he gave his name and date of birth.

A quick check on the PNC of the details he'd given before we drove off, and I discovered he was wanted by the Serious and Organised Crime Agency for a £48-million fraud, the biggest I'd ever had a hand in arresting anyone for. There was even an operation name for his arrest. For a fraud of such magnitude, he was sure to have received a lengthy custodial sentence for that one.

49.

Disruptive Passengers on Aircraft

Continuing with the Heathrow theme for a moment, you'd be surprised as to how many times we're called to disruptive passengers on board aircraft. I've had cabin crew with black eyes after being assaulted by passengers, I've had them spat at (disgusting) and kicked. I even had one passenger who during mid-flight had tried to open one of the doors (impossible by the way, don't worry if you see someone doing the same on your holiday flight) and had used so much force he had actually bent the metal door handle up at an angle. When I turned up, he was sat in his seat, totally immobile because the crew had wrapped him up, around and around his body repeatedly, with cling film! Unreal!

I've had passengers who I've found lying on the toilet floor with their hands and feet bound together with zip-ties and even had a bit of a fight with a drunk Norwegian Commando who had hit a member of the cabin crew.

What is really funny, and this has happened quite a few times, is when you take these people off the aircraft (often in handcuffs) the rest of the passengers all together cheer you on and clap and say, 'Well done officer!' That never happened during any street arrests. It must be a big relief for them to finally have these often loud, drunk and obnoxious individuals that they've been forced to listen to, sometimes for hours, finally removed from the aircraft.

One time we met an aircraft where on board were three armed American air marshals, who had stopped a guy after he began banging on the cockpit door demanding entry. They had bent him over a seat and had just held him down there until the aircraft had landed. They said he had gone quiet and no wonder – he had suffered a heart attack whilst being held down for so long. Luckily he survived this and lucky too for the air marshals I guess.

I arrested an older Egyptian man for doing something similar once, trying to force his way into the cockpit by trying to smash down the door. It was never going to happen of course, but he gave it his best shot until he was jumped on by staff and passengers.

Almost exactly a year later to the day, I'm called to yet another disruptive passenger and lo and behold it's the same Egyptian gentleman, doing exactly the same thing on the same airline! As I'm dealing with him I tell him it was me who dealt with him and arrested him a year ago on the very same flight. It was like he'd met an old friend; he was so pleased to see me! He warmly shook my hand, came willingly when I arrested him and even a few days later dropped a big tin of Cadbury Roses at the police station front counter for me! Trouble was I'd been off for a few days and someone had opened the tin and scoffed most of them. That's theft that is!

I never did find out why he tried it twice. Probably didn't know himself. The effect of in-flight drinks and prescribed medication!

50.

The Day I Started Not to Care

I had nicked someone for a theft of some sort, which isn't that unusual I know, but upon dealing with him back at the station, checks showed he had a huge list of previous convictions as long as your arm for all manner of crimes. It was strange no one had ever heard of him, until he told me he had only recently moved into the area from another part of London.

Over the course of the next couple of years our paths crossed a few times, but it was the last time I ever had any dealings with him that sticks in my mind. A call had come out to his address, made by him, saying that there were two men outside his door who were there, he thought, to kill him.

There had been no suggestion of any weapons seen, so I put myself up for the call and knowing exactly where he lived and the quickest way there, I was on scene fairly quickly. Now if you're ever driving to a call where there are suspects present, you don't want the two-tones blaring out giving the game away; you want a relatively silent approach otherwise you're never going to catch people 'in the act', so for the last part, you want them turned off. It's a judgement call as to when you do it.

I arrived on scene first, followed by another pair of officers close behind me. The pavement area outside the front door that led up to the flat was fairly wide and had one large, long, raised brick-built flower bed outside it, with large shrubs growing in them. This partly obscured the view of the two men I could see standing outside the informant's front door, who had turned to face us when we arrived. As I got out they made no attempt to run and as I approached the man nearest to me, I could see by his feet something wrapped up in a yellow duster, the sort you do your housework with.

My colleague went and secured the other guy and we separated them and began to ask them about why they were there. As we were doing this, another officer looked at this item lying on the ground wrapped up in the duster and it was a handgun (later to be forensically examined and found to be genuine, with live rounds in the magazine).

Other officers who were looking around where the other guy was being spoken to, found another similar live handgun, also wrapped in a yellow duster, pushed into the shrubs in the raised flower bed outside the front door.

They were both arrested for possession of a firearm with the intent to endanger life and both ended up sometime down the line with court dates set at the local Crown Court.

Now when I say it's the time I started not to care, it wasn't the job or the people it was my duty to protect

I didn't care about, it was seeing the results of court cases I didn't care about anymore.

It was the seemingly endless deal making between the prosecution and the defence; 'If you reduce the charge to this lesser offence, then my client will plead guilty to it,' etc., thus saving the cost and time of a trial. It seemed to happen a lot.

On this occasion, a pre-trial review was held at the court, which isn't something I was too familiar with, not something we'd ever get involved in really. It's when a case may be deemed complex or could be going on for some time; the parties get together and any areas of dispute are identified and narrowed down to make the trial run smoother (got to thank Google again for that one!)

The sticking point, or should I say argument made by the defence in this case was as follows. The guns we recovered, although at the feet of the suspects, were not actually seen in their hands. That's true; I couldn't tell a lie. Forensic examination of the guns revealed that the suspects' DNA was indeed on the outside of the weapons.

The bullets in the weapons, however, did not have the suspects' DNA on them.

The suspects' argument was that they, because of the lifestyles they led, did mix with the sort of people who were criminals and had access to firearms. They could have easily been in the same room as these guns at some point and sneezed, putting their DNA on them. As their DNA was not on any of the bullets, they didn't load the guns or take them to the scene of their arrest, was the argument.

At the end of the day this argument stood up, the defence folded and it was case dismissed before it had ever reached trial at court with a jury to decide the outcome.

From that day on I never wanted to know any court result of any job I did. My job was to nick them and get them off the streets, hand them over to the subsequent investigation team and after that forget about it. It's that court results part I didn't care about anymore. I still cared very much when it came to getting these people off the streets, and protecting the innocent members of the public.

Sometimes I really don't know how defence solicitors can sleep at night. A lot of the time they know their client is guilty; they're just there to lessen the punishment given, by describing or embellishing some bullshit sob story, or do their best to try and make the police look incompetent. They're my most hated profession of any out there.

I wonder if these hired heavies ever went on to do damage to other people when they should have been languishing at Her Majesty's pleasure?

51.

How'd They Miss?

Of all the places to commit an armed robbery, why would anyone choose a bloody off-licence? Well these two did and they held the place up at gunpoint whilst they emptied the till.

The staff had pressed an alarm button situated under the counter, which ended up coming out over our radios as a Central Station Panic Alarm, always a good shout, especially at a commercial premises. A colleague of mine had arrived first, quite soon after the alarm call had come out actually and had stated over the radio he had seen the suspects and that he was chasing them on foot. They had entered a park just a road away and as I parked up and ran into the park some way behind my friend, one of the suspects stopped, turned and fired two shots at him, neither hitting him, or me some way behind.

How they missed him was beyond me, as he was a big lump of a guy.

We continued with the foot chase and lost them near a busy dual carriageway. Luckily other officers had positioned

159

themselves over in that direction, thinking that's where the suspects could have been heading. Anyway to cut a long story short (at last I hear you say), the pair were eventually arrested by other officers after they were seen by them running over a main road and into the gardens of a line of houses there.

A handgun was retrieved from one of them, as later were the two spent cartridge cases from where they had fired at my mate, along with a bag containing the cash stolen from the till. All in all, a nice tidy little job.

I think they both got a good few years in jail for that one.

52.

Chases

It's always great chasing suspects, even better to catch them. I was going to say it's 'fun' to chase suspects, but I wouldn't want to belittle the victims of the crimes that these individuals are running from, because it sure as hell isn't fun for them, that much is blatantly obvious.

You've got to understand that one of the reasons people join the police is to catch criminals and the chase and detention of these types is the icing on the cake of what policing is all about. Well, to me it is anyway.

I've chased drug dealers across a golf course with the police helicopter above and when we weren't gaining much ground on them, the helicopter swooped down and almost touching the ground, flared up in front of the suspects, making them stop and thereby giving us the chance to grab hold of them and arrest them.

Once after a chase involving a stolen car, I leapt out and dragged the driver out of the car, after smashing his window with my baton. He was struggling to get away, but not fighting as such. After I'd handcuffed him on the ground, my phone rang. I answered it as I was pinning this suspect to the ground and had a brief conversation with my brother, saying I was a bit busy as I was sitting on top of a car thief at that moment in time and that I'd call him back. Funny.

I've jumped out of a window of a police station control room once, after an Inspector was calling for urgent assistance as he tackled a group of street robbers nearby, only to be the first on scene with him and taking one of them down hard onto the ground and nicking him after a short chase (anything to get out of that control room, eh!)

One time I'd taken a call to an elderly lady being robbed in the street. I was on scene pretty quickly and found she had been pushed to the ground, breaking one of her legs in the process and the man responsible had ripped her handbag from her grasp and had run off down the road.

I actually saw him moments later from the description given and started to try and chase him down on foot. I wasn't gaining much ground on him, bearing in mind all the kit we carry, body armour and boots etc, up against him in jeans and trainers. It was during this chase I saw two young lads up ahead of me and I shouted at them to follow him and keep eyes on him, to try and see where he goes. They were only very young teenagers, but pegged it off after this man.

When I turned a corner, blowing out of my backside, I saw the two young lads were stopped, and they were pointing to a parked car. 'He's under there,' they called out to me. There he was lying under this parked car. I grabbed him hard by the scruff of his neck and unceremoniously dragged him out from under there, handcuffing him behind his back while telling him what I thought of him. Not printable here I fear. The lady's handbag was recovered too by a dog handler, having been thrown by the suspect over a garden wall during the foot chase.

Interestingly, the suspect I arrested was later charged with a string of other similar offences, all robbing the elderly of their handbags. One sad aspect was something I later found about the victim. Doctors who had treated her at the hospital had only given her maybe a year to live, such was the seriousness of not only the break to her leg that we knew about, but she had badly broken her hip during the robbery too. That coupled with her age, the doctors feared, wasn't a good combination for her future life expectancy. He got a custodial sentence though, which was something I suppose.

As a thank you to the two young lads, I recommended them for, and they received, Chief Superintendent's Commendations for their brave spirited actions in helping detain a robbery suspect.

There have been too many vehicle chases to put any down in real detail here; they're all much of a muchness really. Some stand out because they go on for some time, some because of the arrest at the end of it.

One vehicle that I was pursuing which had ended up crashing into railings near Wembley Stadium stands out. I had completed a check on the dodgy looking car and driver as it drove along the road, and received the information back that a man who uses the car was wanted for a murder. A pursuit commenced, as it became obvious that he certainly didn't want to be stopped by police. I had the helicopter above me towards the end of the chase (call sign India 99) and after the vehicle crashed into railings at the end of a dead-end road, the driver had then run across a six-lane wide main road, vaulting the central reservation fence (closely followed by myself) and had then jumped a fence or two by some houses, and had hidden behind a shed in one of the gardens. The helicopter directed me onto him, and he was arrested by myself after a minor tussle, because he was indeed the man wanted for the murder. Lovely.

Another that stands out was a chase involving a white van that had gone on for some time, through about three different police grounds. It had started in the dark and didn't end until the sun had come up. The van came to a crashing halt in the centre of Hammersmith Broadway and I'll never forget, as I leapt out of the passenger seat of our car, looking up to see the helicopter banking over in a steep turn right above us against the then clear blue sky, as we rushed forward to detain the occupants.

Had an unusual one in the snow once. A good friend had put out on the radio late at night, while it was still snowing, that while out on patrol he had come across a few parked-up vans where someone had wiped the snow off the side windows. Theft of tools, especially from parked vans overnight, is a big thing. It also means the owners are having part of their livelihoods stolen – no tools means no work; no work means no income for the household bills. It really is a shitty crime to commit.

I made my way to where he was and we started to see other parked-up vans with snow wiped off their windows. And I know it sounds like it's made up, but we tracked the suspect doing this by following his footprints in the snow. We eventually caught up with him and he was off on his toes. We chased after him on foot, just following his footprints in the snow. We went up and over a couple of garden walls and fences, before the footprints went up and through someone's back garden, to a dead end where he couldn't get out because of a very high gate. We lifted up a fence panel that was leaning against the side of the house and there he was, sat under there all crouched up, breathing heavily. He was searched and found to be in possession of one of those large red-handled glass hammers used to smash vehicle glass in an emergency. He was arrested for 'Going equipped for theft'; chiefly theft from vans.

What was infuriating about this job, was that he was left for an early turn unit to deal with, one from the ground where he had eventually been arrested (he was arrested on another police station's 'area', not our own). When we came back in that night, we found out he had been released without charge. Let go in other words. When my mate made enquiries with the officer who had interviewed and dealt with him, he said the suspect stated in the interview that he had been out that night just having a snowball fight with friends and that was why he had been wiping snow from vans. And the glass hammer? Just a tool from his place of work he happened to have on him. At 2 o'clock in the morning.

We were furious! God some people are just bloody useless. Or lazy? Maybe both.

53.

Grenfell

On the 14th June 2017, a fire swept through a tower block called Grenfell, situated in North Kensington, a fact that I'm sure every reader is all too aware of. 72 people died in total and many lives changed forever. It was the worst fire in a residential property since the Second World War.

Now, in the police we all wear many hats. What I mean by that is you have your regular day job, but you're also trained in all manner of other things, be that Specialist Search, Protestor Removal, Public Order, Driver Training and suchlike. One such role that I was trained in was that of Body Recovery, or to give it its full title, UKDVI – UK Disaster Victim and Identification Unit.

It's the unit involved in recovering and identifying the deceased and human remains, where there are multiple fatalities.

As a trained member of this team for quite some years, I was called upon to assist in the recovery of the deceased from Grenfell Tower and also to assist in the many post mortems held at a Central London mortuary too.

I don't want to dwell on the details of what we all saw there both at the tower and the post-mortems too much, as it is still a very raw experience for both the survivors and the families of the deceased.

Some things do need saying though.

I will say that whatever you saw on the television is nothing compared to when you see it for real, with your own eyes. Every day when I stepped out of Latimer Road tube station and looked up at the burnt out shell of the tower block, it was like being punched in the face; it was so truly horrendous and shocking to see, especially knowing how many had died in there and in fact were still lying in there.

The ferocity of the fire split the sides of the building open on some corners, enough for you to literally poke your arm through. The Fire Brigade assured us though that the structure was sound enough for us all to work in, so that was good enough for me. One thing that became obvious straight away, was the lack of access inside the building. The lifts couldn't be used obviously and all that remained for us and indeed for all the residents that night, was the one single narrow central stairwell.

That truly made you stop and think. That was the one exit point for all those caught up in the events of that night, and the one access point for the fire crews. In fact, I remember vividly the push-buttons on the lift control panels. The heat had made the plastic buttons melt, so they hung downwards like thick spaghetti, each one of them with a floor number disc on the end of it.

I helped recover bodies and body parts from, if I remember correctly, floor 7 right up to the top floor. The most disturbing sight was on floor 17, where in one corner of the room there were 11 bodies piled on top of one another. From full-grown adults to the tiniest of babies, mixed up and piled three-high in places. I won't describe the state they were in; it's not something I wish to revisit.

I spent quite a bit of time on this floor, shifting the huge amounts of debris from their bodies, carefully separating it all so nothing was missed. It took many days to accomplish this.

When we were doing the recoveries (if there was more than a single body found together), you had in your small team a forensic archaeologist, a photographer and a pathologist. This was so that not even the tiniest bit of bone was missed and that the relatives could have as much of their loved ones back as was humanly possible.

I know there had been, at the time, some anger amongst people about the time taken in the recovery process, but they had no idea just how painstaking a process it was. We had to recover every piece of bone, right down to the little phalanx bones at the end of your finger tips and every single tooth and match them up to the bodies they belonged to. And all this had to be dug out of the mounds of debris they were mixed in with, hence the forensic archaeologists we had with us. You'd clear a tiny area at a time, using the smallest of tools such as tweezers similar to what a fine model maker would use, identify the relevant bones or the body parts and then slip a piece of blue paper roll under them so they stood out and wouldn't be missed later. These would be packed or boxed up and labelled accordingly. If it was a full body on its own, that made the job much faster, but having said that, it would still take time to do the job methodically and correctly, so nothing was missed. Items of jewellery, for example, would be photographed and bagged separately, as these would be of huge benefit in identifying the deceased.

There's no dignity in death, but there is certainly dignity in the way the dead can be recovered.

And I'd tell anyone who wanted to know, you wouldn't believe the incredible care and compassion, the lengths we went to, to make sure that the deceased were recovered in full, as much as possible. I think in over 30 years' police work, it's the most satisfying and rewarding work I'd ever done.

Parts of it still haunt me now and I'd much rather forget about certain aspects of it, but I know I never will.

The towels that had been pressed against the front doors to stop smoke coming in were still evident, even though the doors had burnt away to nothing. The vases and money boxes that were still perfectly pristine as though they had just been purchased from a shop and laid amongst the dirty grey debris – remaining shiny and spotless due to them being fired in their manufacture; it made them impervious to more heat – that was a real strange one, quite disturbing.

The plans written on the walls of the ground floor area by the firefighters on the night. Also the smiling face of a bright red Henry the Hoover, staring out at me from a burnt cupboard, that had itself been destroyed by the fire.

It'll haunt me forever.

54.

An Amazing Pair of Tits

The car had hit the high kerb of the central reservation, launched itself up into the air and had come smashing down onto the crash barriers that separated the two opposing carriageways.

Nothing out of the ordinary here I thought, just another accident, no other car involved, just the one lying here bent and broken.

The female passenger had been thrown forward during the impact and her head had struck the windscreen hard, causing what's known as a 'bullseye', where the glass stays intact, but is shattered into a round 'head' shape. Bullseye isn't a disrespectful term in any way, it's an industry standard term used through all the emergency services. It's a good indicator of potential head trauma. There were even long black hairs hanging from the shattered circle of glass that had been pulled from her head as it had impacted the windscreen.

There were a couple of ambulances on scene with the lady passenger in one and the driver in another, as well as a few police officers.

I went to the ambulance with the lady passenger in it and, although she was being taken to hospital due to it being a head injury, I was told it wasn't life-threatening at all. Great news. I then went and got in the back of the ambulance where the driver was sitting having his relatively minor injuries being attended to by the crew. We were having a chat like you do and he seemed like a decent lad. The ambulance crew said it was fine to breathalyse him, so another officer did this and he passed easily; he hadn't been drinking at all. I asked him to tell me what happened, as it appeared to me that his was the only car involved and it was late at night, so the traffic was quite light on the road.

He was totally hands up about what had happened. It was a new girlfriend of his and she had been flirting with him heavily on the drive home. She had undone her seatbelt and pulled her top up to show him what lay underneath.

He said his eyes hadn't been on the road at the time he smashed into the central reservation. 'I couldn't help but stare,' he said. 'She's got an amazing pair of tits!'

55.

Oh No, Not Another Football Match

Being public-order-trained, you'd always find yourself every Saturday, stuck doing football aid during the footie season. To some this was great, but to someone like me who can't stand football, it was as dull as ditch water. If we were posted mostly in the stadiums, which a lot of officers liked, my heart would sink, but if we were posted to the local town, patrolling the pubs and suchlike, now that was a lot more interesting. A bit more 'hands on' shall we say.

My first ever football match I policed was in the infamous 'shed' at Chelsea, a roofed standing terrace behind one of the goals there. Christ, that was an eye-opening experience, walking around in a sea of piss, breaking up fights whilst other supporters tried to stop you!

I remember the last match played at the old Wembley, it was between England and Germany in the year 2000. At half-time it really kicked off behind the terraces, with fans fighting one another and then turning their attention to the police who were trying to keep them apart. There was a big whirling of fists and feet and the occasional baton strike going in. We even had officers from the mounted division who had come in on foot and they joined in the melee too. We had all sorts come flying our way from the back of the crowd, mainly aimed at our heads; anything and everything that wasn't bolted down was thrown at us. When they had finished throwing that lot at us, they started throwing coins instead. When the second half started, they all went back to their seats and I picked up some coins from the floor and made £7 out of it! Cheers!

Once at a QPR match at their home ground, we were policing a match between them and Cardiff. During the briefing, the borough commander for Hammersmith and Fulham told us to be intolerant of any antisocial behaviour and to allow no hooliganism at all from supporters. Because it was Cardiff playing and they had a long history of football hooliganism among their supporters, the extra amount of police resources that were put in place to maintain order was extraordinary. It was the highest number of police officers deployed there in the past six years.

My serial (the one sergeant and five or six PCs) were posted to the divide between the home and the away supporters. The Cardiff supporters were a highly volatile bunch and more than once some tried to scale the very low fence between them and the QPR supporters, with us trying to push them back. As usual the police became the target and we were all stood at the fence line fending off blows from the Cardiff lads who were now intent on getting over the fence for a good fight. Many baton strikes were going in as we kept them at bay, but they still kept coming back for more. I remember locking eyes with a Cardiff bloke who was intent on getting me. He grabbed hold of the fence to jump over and I shouted at him to, 'Get the fuck back,' just a carefully crafted swear word used as a verbal stunning technique to show we really meant business. With this he turned to all the other supporters around him, saying repeatedly, 'That officer swore at me!' He was really outraged by it! Not the multiple baton strikes they'd been receiving or anything, just that an officer had sworn. Madness! At the end of the long day, there had been 62 arrests in total. In fact, that borough commander actually wrote a letter of thanks to our borough commander at Ealing, praising us for a 'job brilliantly done'. Nice to get a pat on the back and have hard work recognised.

During one mad match again at Loftus Road Stadium, I forget who was playing there against QPR, we literally had a running fight with fans before the game, during the game at half-time and then after the game as well. During public-order incidents like these, you can't really go around making arrests, unless it's for a really serious incident. You'll just end up depleting your resources and end up having less and less officers to deal with all the disorder.

When you were finally dismissed from the tour of duty, it always came as such a welcome relief. Once, while waiting for some police officer stragglers to make their way back to our vehicle at Wembley, Frank Carson the Irish comedian jumped on board, totally unplanned and just done on impulse. He proceeded to stand at the front and treat us to a few minutes of his stand-up comedy routine. It was fantastic!

56.

You'd Have to See It to Believe It

It was another call to a possible collapse behind locked doors, but this time the call came from a concerned neighbour who thought she had heard her elderly next door neighbour calling out for help. This informant who had called us didn't have a key for the property, so couldn't gain any access so had dialled 999 instead; the right thing to do.

When we arrived, I opened the letterbox and put my ear to it and called out the lady's name. She made some incoherent reply, so it was obvious she had collapsed, or was ill inside, so I put a swift boot to her front door, breaking it open easily. Now once inside, the sight that greeted me was straight out of TV comedy. In the lady's rather large living room was one of these great big wooden packing crates, the type with the black printed words stamped on the outside of it like you'd see in a cartoon. She had fallen backwards into it somehow and the only thing we could see were her outstretched arms sticking out one side and her outstretched legs the other. We couldn't even see her head!

We rushed forward and ever so gently lifted her up and out of the packing case. As we did so her bones creaked and rubbed together; we could feel them doing so as we lifted her. Apparently, it was a condition called Crepitus, which was a new one for me. She was checked over by the ambulance service, but appeared OK and was left at home with her friendly neighbour. I'll never forget the sight of her sticking out of that crate though!

That reminds me of another time we were called upon to help the ambulance service, who needed to gain access to an elderly lady who had called them. This particular lady had a bit of a weird obsession, so the crew told me who had dealt with her many times before. She was obsessed with her own, to put it politely, faeces. They said she'd sit at home with her fingers up there, trying to get every bit of excrement out she could, even using spoons to assist her. That's one when I didn't bother going into the house after I'd forced the door for them. I was staying outside for that one! Which makes me think, I don't think I ever asked, 'What does she do with it when she's got it out?' Next...

57.

Choose Your Time Wisely...

A Securicor team were transporting a single lone prisoner from a court to a prison when he had become violent in the back of the van. He had managed to kick the door of his small holding cell, where he had been sitting, off its hinges, and had assaulted one of the guards sitting in the vehicle, as well as causing yet more damage to the inside of the van – even though he was handcuffed at the time. The guards had dialled 999 and were told of their nearest police station and to drive straight there. A 'reception committee' of police officers was arranged to meet the crew in the back yard of the station and the crew were kept on the phone by the operator. When they neared the station, the doors to the back yard were opened and they were able to drive straight in.

(A reception committee is just a figure of speech; it just means to have some officers waiting in the rear yard, as someone is coming in with a prisoner who is a real handful and needs more than just a couple of officers to deal with them.)

The rear yard was a much more secure and sterile location to deal with the incident, rather than just parking outside in the street and dealing with it there.

Once the vehicle had stopped, the dazed and quite scared crew got out and told us that the prisoner was inside the van, just sat back in the seat, very angry, very big and extremely volatile.

Now, it's no good in that situation to just rush forward and try and grab him; people would just get hurt, us as well as him, and at the end of the day nobody wants that. It's also no good a group going and trying to reason with him, as that would just wind him up further. Far better for one officer to do this with just one voice and one face to deal with. I've found that people respond far better to this type of approach.

So I approached the van, with a friend standing a short distance behind me, who is a highly experienced and wise officer and also happens to be a lump of a PC who's great to have with you if it all goes wrong.

I start talking quietly to the prisoner in the back of the van, explaining the situation and the fact that what has happened has got to be dealt with; there's no getting away from the fact. He appeared full of hate and was a very angry man indeed. He made it quite clear he wasn't going anywhere, so it was just a case of trying to keep chipping away at him, not getting angry or aggressive myself, just keeping the tone low and at all times appearing reasonable.

The line that won the day was me telling him that he had to go into the police station one way or another and that if he walked in with me, I wouldn't hold on to him or anything like that. I'd let him walk in with his head held high, like a man, by my side. That or get carried in, the choice was his.

He gave it a few seconds thought and agreed to walk in with me. He got up and out of the van and as he did so, he walked by my side, with my other friend also walking with us. As we crossed the yard, one of the other officers who was a part of this reception committee came forward and started to say the words, 'You're under arrest for...'

'NOOOO,' my friend and I said together! Now was certainly not the time for that!

Anyway, he was walked into the custody area, straight into a cell and the door shut. Once he was safely in there and not a danger to anyone, that's when my friend could come forward and arrest him for any offences he deemed suitable.

There's always a time and a place...

58.

Rank is No Indication of Ability or Common Sense…

I think the heading here says it all; everyone's seen it before and I think the basic premise applies to every working profession out there, of that I'm sure most of us would agree.

This leads me on to a call I attended a long time ago now, where we had received a call from a young woman who had come home to find her female flatmate lying on the floor in a pool of blood. She was very distraught of course and in a state of shock as most of us would be. Several officers had turned up at the address, but of course you don't all go trampling in there, in case it's a crime scene. On the flip side of that, you've got to get in there quickly in case any first aid has to be given; after all, we don't know if the woman is still alive or not. It's a fine balancing act. You also don't want a load of size 11s possibly destroying any vital evidence. You've got to decide who goes in and establish what's called a common approach path. That means that whoever subsequently goes into the house as part of any ongoing investigation, follows the exact route you've taken, because if they don't, you may well have all piled in there regardless anyway.

I walk into the house first, with a colleague behind me holding a first aid kit. I walk down the hallway, keeping tight to one side and following the directions given by the lady as to where her flatmate was situated, I step over the hallway carpet into the last open door on the left which is the kitchen.

There lying face down on the kitchen floor was her flatmate. She was fully clothed but lying in a pool of blood that appeared to be coming from what I'd guessed was a head injury. There were a few items scattered on the floor that seemed to have possibly been knocked off the kitchen worktop. The worrying thing was that among these few items lying on the floor, such as a broken bowl and a magazine, was, more worryingly, a small kitchen knife.

What's more, the kitchen back door was wide open, and led out into a very small garden, and just behind the garden was a busy dual carriageway.

Even to the untrained or inexperienced eye, this screamed crime scene. At some point during all this an ambulance had been requested and they confirmed to me what we had thought; she had indeed passed away and there was nothing they could do for her at all.

In situations like this, the CID are requested to attend the scene of course and the investigation snowballs. It's essentially out of your hands now, you've done your bit and the house is now treated as a crime scene.

Now, before the arrival of any CID to the house, my Inspector turns up. He's not my favourite person in the world; I used to just find him inefficient and seemingly incapable at making good policing decisions. He was certainly no leader and I always viewed him as a pretty inadequate police officer. Let's just say he inspired no confidence in me if he ever turned up at a scene.

But at this scene he did turn up, having been requested to attend – after all, he was the Duty Inspector at the time. I talked him through the information we had received so far as I walked him along the common approach path through the house. We stopped just shy of the kitchen, just enough so he could look inside and see the woman lying there. I explained about the flatmate coming home to find her friend lying there in the kitchen, about her young age, that she had no medical issues we were aware of, the fact she was lying in a pool of blood, about the knife on the floor and the fact that the kitchen door was wide open, leading out to the main road outside.

He crossed his arms and put his chin in his hand as if thinking deeply. He turned to me and said, 'So what makes you think it's suspicious?'

Honestly, if you've got to ask that question in those circumstances, you need to have a long hard chat with yourself.

Luckily the CID were in full agreement with me on this one and it was treated as a murder scene.

It was at the subsequent post mortem some time later that it was discovered she had suffered some kind of seizure as a result of an undiagnosed brain tumour, the poor girl. She had just collapsed in her kitchen and hit the floor head first causing secondary injuries to her face and head and dropping whatever she had been holding at the time.

Incredibly sad, but it still doesn't defend the remark made by the Inspector!

59.

More CPR and Missing my 50th Birthday Drinks

It was less than an hour to go before the end of my shift and I was all set to shoot home, get changed quickly and go out with the family for drinks to celebrate my 50th birthday. It was all planned and I was watching the minutes tick by. Then, of course, the one call comes out you just can't avoid.

An American Airlines flight had taken off from Heathrow, bound for Chicago. It was over an hour into its flight when one of the passengers on board had suffered a heart attack and the aircraft was turning around and coming back to the airport. We were told what stand they were going to put the aircraft on and a few of us went there to await the arrival of the aircraft, which we were now told was only minutes from landing. We were met at the stand by two paramedic units and some of the airline ground crew, who were being passed messages from the crew on board the aircraft.

They had stated that the crew had stopped giving the passenger CPR, as he had passed away. The aircraft landed, taxied to the stand as planned and we all boarded en masse. We were directed down to the very back part of the aircraft, just past the last bulkhead. There, lying on the floor, was an elderly gent wearing blue jeans, but with his shirt cut off. He had a small defibrillator attached to him and although the crew had stopped giving CPR, he was actually still being worked on by two doctors and a nurse who had been on board. Defibrillators are carried on most aircraft as part of their standard first aid equipment.

The gentleman's family were all on board: his wife, his brother and his sister-in-law. They were ushered away from the scene, as it must have been incredibly upsetting for them, and sat a bit further up the aircraft, as seats became available when the other passengers were disembarked.

One of the cabin crew told me they had heard shouts of 'man down, man down' from another flight attendant and saw the elderly gent slumped down onto his knees and then fall onto his back. This member of cabin crew had commenced CPR straight away, while another had contacted the pilot to inform them of what had happened.

And yes, just like in the films, the pilot had made an announcement over the PA system, asking if there were any doctors on board the flight and to make themselves known. And as luck would have it two stepped forward and a nurse.

I stepped in and took over the chest compressions at the request of one of the paramedics who had boarded the flight with me. While the other paramedics went about their life-saving work, another paramedic and myself alternated between chest compressions and rescue breaths into the man's airway. We did this continually for 45 minutes which, let me assure you, is sweaty, exhausting work.

Other officers were looking after the family, getting their details, obtaining statements from the two doctors and the nurse and also the cabin crew directly involved. It's important to get this right away for any later report to the Coroner. It's no good, when you need a statement later, to find your witnesses are on the other side of the world.

Twice the paramedics thought they had a pulse and twice they said it had gone. It was incredibly impressive to watch them at work, such is their professionalism. One thing that really impressed me while I was doing the chest compressions, was watching them screw a metal cannula into the man's tibia bone in his lower leg. They couldn't get a suitable vein in his body to use to inject any drugs into, so this cannula, screwed directly into the bone, meant they could now get drugs into the blood supply that was running through the man's bone marrow.

I'm sorry to say the man passed away and the advanced paramedic on scene pronounced life extinct at 7.18pm.

This set the wheels in motion for the deceased to be removed from the aircraft and after informing the Coroner's Officer, undertakers were called and they arrived at the aircraft a little before 9pm.

By this time the family had all been removed to the airline's lounge and after that taken to one of the more upmarket airport hotels to make any arrangements they needed to. I can't imagine how traumatic an event that must have been for the family, especially the wife. I've actually dealt with other similar events on aircraft, some where it's just the partner with the deceased and no other family. It's heartbreaking.

Obviously I never made the birthday celebrations, but that pales into insignificance really doesn't it?

60.

Lend Me Your Ear...

I was the second to arrive at the scene of a fight between two brothers at a small house on an estate in West London. The house was in a right state when I arrived and I think they must have bounced off every object in every room in the downstairs of the house. There was a lady in the kitchen, wailing and sobbing her heart out, who turned out to be the mother of the two lads, who were both in their late teens to maybe 20 years of age. There was a lot of blood too and one of the brothers, the injured one, was sitting on the sofa in the living room.

He had been stabbed a fair few times, nothing puncturing any major organs, just stab wounds to his upper arms. He was yelling out and was in the process of having wound dressings applied by one of the officers present while waiting for an ambulance to arrive. He was holding one of his arms up to the side of his head and when he took it away, you could see he had the vast majority of one of his ears cut clean off.

The brother who had done this was just lying on the floor, screaming and crying. The mother told me he was schizophrenic, as well as having other mental health issues. What with him, the yelling brother and the wailing mother, it was quite the chaotic scene.

As other officers arrived, they detained the other brother. Knowing a very brief history of his mental illnesses, he still had to be nicked, after all he had stabbed his brother multiple times with a kitchen knife and cut off a damn good portion of an ear.

As officers walked him out of the house, the mother was in bits. It was one of those rare times – she desperately needed comforting and turned to me to bury her weeping face in my shoulder. I reacted instinctively and put my arm around her to reassure her that everything would be OK, and to just give it time. I'll never forget how thankful she was that we showed so much care towards both of her sons. Sometimes you've got to come down on criminals like a tonne of bricks; sometimes you've just got to have that empathy with people and put your arm around them. I wouldn't make a habit of it, but you've got to care.

Stabbings are certainly no rarity on the streets of London. But certainly not all make worthy news stories. I think the most we had on a single night duty shift was four separate unrelated stabbings, with one of them being a murder.

I remember one stabbing I went to and the victim was a Lithuanian man. He had a deep stab wound to his side, but just brushed it off as 'nothing'. Made of different stuff these East European guys.

One thing I will say to anyone reading this who is thinking about joining the police – if you ever find someone after a call to a fight or a robbery or anything like that who is injured but doesn't seem to care about it or want to know, there's a damn good chance that they're actually the suspect.

You just haven't found the victim yet.

61.

Cheers For Being So Predictable

Females will always get attention from men; after all if they didn't the human population would grind to a halt. But if that attention is unwarranted or makes the woman feel uncomfortable, then that is where they've overstepped the line and it becomes unacceptable. That's when a bit of action is called for; after all, I'm married and have a daughter. How would I like it if they were receiving attention that made them feel uncomfortable? I'd be out there trying to sort out whoever had done it; it's as simple as that.

There was a girl's school on one of my old grounds and I was asked one day if I'd go along and speak to the head there, as some of the girls had been on the end of some suggestive remarks from some men, that made them feel very uncomfortable. I went along and spoke with both the head and some of the girls involved. They explained that they were regularly approached by these same men in the park and how the men were always in the same area drinking; it was their regular haunt if you like.

They couldn't say exactly what man was saying what, it was just a barrage of sexual remarks coming from them all. I went to the location in the park where the girls said the men congregated, but they weren't there.

Now it's all well and good having a degree in hindsight, but I've always thought it better to have a degree in foresight. See where the road is heading, see any issues that might need addressing in the future and sort them out before they materialise into actual problems.

With this in mind, I arranged to go and see the Sergeant of the local Safer Neighbourhood Team, which in a nutshell is the new name for a Homebeat Officer, if you're old enough to remember them. I passed on all the information to him and hoped the problem could get sorted, hoping that the team would patrol the area and nip the problem in the bud.

It was actually 11 days later, when a call had come out on the radio that three schoolgirls had been indecently assaulted in the very same park. I wasn't able to attend due to being stuck dealing with another job, but I was able to direct those officers who were making their way there, to where the suspects might be, based upon the girls telling me where the men always hung out. They were indeed found at that spot and it resulted in four arrested by the attending officers for indecent assault.

Now, the problem wasn't fixed as such before any crime had been committed, we can't be everywhere at once, such is the demand on officers. But having a group of men taken off the streets for indecent assault, on schoolgirls too, that's a damn fine result in my book.

62.

No, I'm Not Arresting Him Guv'

It seemed a simple enough request from my team Inspector, who had chosen me specifically for the job in hand, as we had known one another since we were PCs together when she had first joined the job and she trusted my judgement.

Can I go along to Hammersmith Hospital and arrest a man who was there as a patient for the attempted murder of his wife? He had tried to strangle her with a dressing gown cord apparently and I don't know how, but the investigating team had got wind that he was in this hospital now as a patient and rather than go and make the arrest themselves, they had asked if we had anyone available to go and make the collar on their behalf. Now to me, the reason they asked us was, if he was in there for an extended period, they wouldn't have to sit around on their arses waiting for him to be discharged.

Still, it didn't bother me, it sounded an interesting job and I was more than up for it. When I arrived on the ward, I discovered that he had been admitted because he had suffered a heart attack out on the street somewhere and passers-by had called for an ambulance and now here he was.

He had survived the episode, but was still very ill, but conscious in a bed on one of the wards. There was no way on earth I was going to go and arrest him when he's in that condition. Can you imagine being cross-examined in court over that, or if the papers ever got hold of it? 'So, officer, you arrested this man while he was lying in hospital after suffering a heart attack?' It just wasn't going to happen, no way. That would have been a bad judgement call. I'm sure the nursing staff wouldn't have let me anyway.

I contacted my boss and explained the situation, telling her that he wasn't going to be arrested. Not then anyway. A short time later, my boss called me back, saying that this Detective Inspector was jumping up and down in a rage, demanding I arrest this man, so that various swabs and scrapings could be obtained from his hands, etc.

I told her it just wasn't going to happen. I wasn't going to be the one to cause him to have another heart attack. (Mind you, if he did have one he was in the right place!)

While hanging around the ward, by chance I happened to meet the cardiologist who was at that time the doctor in charge of the suspect's treatment. I explained my situation to him and he said that any shock to the suspect could well bring on a much stronger and fatal cardiac arrest and he would never have let me do it. Up to that point, I had only seen the suspect at a distance anyway; he didn't even know I was there.

A short while later, I received a phone call from none other than this Detective Inspector himself. He was annoyed that I wouldn't arrest the suspect and admitted to being angry at my boss (the same rank as him, Inspector – the Detective part means nothing rank-wise) for fully backing me up. I explained the situation, although he was well aware anyway I'm sure and I offered to put the cardiologist on the phone to him, which he declined. Good job too, as they'd just gone home!

The upshot was he was required to send one of his own officers down, to sit on the ward for as long as it took for the suspect to be deemed fit to be spoken to, which could have been many days indeed. And to be honest, I think us going down there first saved the job from a lot of embarrassment further down the line, should the worst have ever happened.

63.

Just a Bit Busy Right Now

One of the grounds I worked on had the third busiest control room in the Metropolitan Police area. I think it was beaten by two police stations in the heart of London's West End in terms of the number of calls it handled.

It was a Saturday afternoon and I had come in to work a late shift, which was 3pm until 11pm. I knew I was posted to our control room and when I went and sat down I saw it had been a really busy day, as there were 45 unassigned calls waiting to be dealt with. That's 45 people who couldn't be dealt with over the phone, but needed an actual police response. None were graded with the 'I - Immediate' response required, they were all marked as 'S', which means 'Soon'. It was still pretty unusual. There were five of us working in the control room that day: three police officers and two civilian members of staff.

Now, don't go jumping to any conclusions here; the civilian operators were absolutely superb, in fact better than the police officers in a way, because this was their bread-and-butter. We were only posted in there occasionally. The actual civilian controller in there, the boss if you like, was at the top of his game and I wouldn't want anyone else in charge in there with me.

We thought it was busy when we started, but within just 45 minutes we had four totally separate firearm incidents running at the same time. I'd never heard of anything like this before. You always get the odd call where someone's been threatened with a gun, but to be dealing with four at once was unheard of.

We had to split the main radio channels into two separate channels and have two operators on each one of these, both running two incidents. Sounds a bit complicated saying it like that. The workload during this was pretty intense, running the incidents on one computer screen, doing Cris and Crimint checks on another (Cris and Crimint were just the names of the computer systems where crimes were recorded and intelligence gathered respectively, to put it in simple terms). RVPs (rendezvous points – a safe location not too far from the incident, but close enough to be effective should officers need to be deployed quickly. Officers can attend here, whether they be local units, dog handlers, ARVs etc.) were established at two of the incidents; the others not requiring them for one reason or another. It was so unusual, we actually had the Chief Superintendent and a Chief Inspector come down from their top floor offices to witness what was going on and keep up-to-date with developments.

We ended up, once everything had calmed down, with one of the calls having a firearm recovered and one man arrested (if I remember correctly, it was a small handgun). Another one was a foot chase by some of our Robbery Squad, with a suspect lost after they had vaulted numerous fences and a wall, but a magazine was recovered with live rounds in that had apparently come from a small submachine gun. The other two resulted in a man arrested for 'Threatening Behaviour' and the last just an intelligence report put onto the police computer system. All in all, it was a very busy shift.

What I remember clearly, is at the end of the day when it was time to hand over to the oncoming night shift, we handed over 15 calls graded as 'I', which as I explained means an immediate police response is required, that's not even counting any calls graded as 'Soon'.

You just can't open a new box of officers; you've only got a finite amount of resources at your disposal and you can't work them into the ground; after all, the next day it'll be me back out there doing the job with them.

64.

Run-of-the-Mill Everyday Arrest (short story!)

Going through some of the piles and piles of subject matter I've accrued over a couple of decades in the planning of this book, so many don't really warrant any inclusion in here. It's because they're so commonplace as to just be an everyday occasion for police officers up and down the land really. An example of what I mean is coming across an accident at a road junction – the driver had overcooked it and stuffed the car into the high kerb, buckling a wheel and bursting a tyre. 'Yeah, so what?' I hear you say. I know what you mean, but a quick check on the PNC on the registration number of the car revealed it had been stolen in a burglary several days earlier. I got someone in the control room to do a check for any description of the burglar and, lo and behold, there had been a bit of a tussle with the house owner during the burglary, which is pretty rare really. He had supplied a brief description of the suspect, which included a tattoo on one of his hands, which matched the man we had there!

The driver was grabbed by the arm before I told him this so he didn't have a chance to run off and he was quickly arrested and cautioned for burglary.

I've got loads of examples like this, but after a while they'd get pretty boring I reckon.

65.

I Don't Remember This One

It's funny really; you deal with just so much over the course of a career, you can't remember everything. Laid out in front of me now I have a copy of what is called a 'Quality of Service Report'. It's a report, typed out this time by a team Inspector, to bring to the Chief Superintendent's attention work of a particularly high standard, worthy of notice.

The details on it state it is for 'outstanding leadership, organisation, common sense and sound judgement at a fast-time firearms incident'.

It details the actions of two officers, myself and a close friend, when we attended a call to a male who had been stabbed in the head and buttocks in North West London. Only when we arrived, did we discover that he had been shot at three times as well.

It says we cordoned off the crime scene, directed other officers to do the house-to-house enquiries, made all the initial arrest enquires using information gained from the victim and other speedy intelligence checks and that we both briefed the ARV units, this particular Inspector and the CID when they arrived on scene. Damn, we sounded busy!

It was purely as a result of our actions, it says, that the male suspect was arrested for attemtped murder, and a replica firearm was recovered from him.

And do you know what, it rings no bells with me; I've completely forgotten about this one. My friend remembers it a bit, but me? Haven't got a Scooby!

66.

More Guns Taken off the Streets

It was a nice spring afternoon when a call came out over the radio to a man in a pub who was in possession of a firearm.

The informant to this happened to be a former Israeli soldier, who was now living in London. He had been in a pub in the local High Street and thought he had seen another man in there briefly show what he was certain was a gun, to another man sat next to him. He had swiftly finished his drink and had left the pub and once a short distance from it, he had dialled 999.

I took the call and my control room arranged for this informant to meet me at the back gates of the police station, which just happened to be at the end of the High Street where this pub was. The call had generated quite a bit of interest and one of our plain clothed Robbery Squad units came and met me at the back gates too. If this male was in the pub and did indeed have a gun, it was vitally important to get him detained and stopped in the quickest time possible, but also in the safest way possible too. No one wants people to get hurt.

We also requested an ARV unit to the back of the station too, but were told that none were available at that time; they were all tucked up on other jobs. That posed a problem, as they are by far the best asset to use in these situations.

The informant arrived quite quickly and introduced himself. He said he was a former soldier in the Israeli Defence Force and 'knew what a gun looked like'. I certainly had no reason to doubt him; after all, he was trying to help us. I got a detailed description of the suspect from him and exactly where he was sitting in the pub, who was around him the last time he saw him, whether he was sitting with easy access either side of him, or was he sat part up against a wall etc.?

The Robbery unit was made up of three plain clothed officers at the time and they volunteered for one of them to casually go into the pub and conduct a bit of fast-time reconnaissance. He was driven up there, dropped off and came back over the radio with the info that the suspect was indeed still sat in the pub, seemingly alone. This officer stayed in there to keep an eye on the suspect and it was now he who was best placed to quickly identify the suspect should other officers enter to detain him.

Once again we were told that there wasn't at that time an armed unit to assist us, so the Robbery Squad decided to go in and detain the guy sitting in there; after all he could leave at any time and go out into the public area. To a degree he was contained in the place he was now and wouldn't really have been in a position to escape. This

206

course of action was agreed by the Duty Inspector also, so with his authority we hurriedly got a couple of marked police vehicles not too far away from the pub, but parked out of sight around a corner and the Robbery Squad made their way up to the pub. At this time one of the ARV units became available and made their way towards the pub in question as quickly as possible. It was while waiting for the armed support to arrive that two of the plain clothes officers watched the suspect in the pub take a small black handgun out from his coat pocket and transfer it around to his back trouser pocket. Game on then.

Obviously I wasn't there for the arrest, but the ARV unit entered the pub, the suspect was identified to them by the Robbery Squad officers already in there and he was detained safely, with no danger caused to anyone.

He was indeed found to be in possession of a loaded firearm and was nicked for this. A gun was taken off the streets and probably a life was saved somewhere down the line. Isn't it great when a plan comes together?

67.

Attempted Murder

There was a block of flats, three floors high, well known to most local officers, that sat on their own just back from a very busy main road with its own little service road running along the front of it. We had often been called to one of the flats there for various domestic assaults over the years. The couple that lived there had each been arrested on past occasions for assaults on one another, but had always come back together as a couple. Thank God I wasn't one of their neighbours!

There was a couple walking along the pavement on the main road where the flats were, but on the other side of the dual carriageway to where they were situated. They had heard over the traffic noise, the sounds of what they described as a woman 'screaming hysterically,' who was chasing a male on the second floor balcony that ran around the entire floor. They could see she was holding what appeared to them to be a large knife and watched as she dropped it over the balcony to the ground below, as the man collapsed onto the floor.

The couple witnessing this had dialled 999 and were relaying to the police operator what they were seeing. They saw the woman run out from the block, run across the ground floor service road outside it and then run back up and go into her second floor flat. There was no brick wall around each floor, just a series of metal railings and the informants said they could see the male just lying there and that someone had come out of one of the other flats and seemed to be trying to help him.

Several of us were making our way to this call, some directed to go straight to the block of flats and this injured man, and some to go and meet the witnesses, who were still on the phone to the police.

I was one of the officers that went to the flats and, as some other officers attended to the injured man, who was bleeding quite badly from a stab wound to his upper body, I was talked along the balcony to the flat that the woman had run back into and yes, it was the very same flat officers had been to in the past. The beige-coloured front door was wide open, so we made our way inside to find a woman sitting in there matching the clothing description given by the very helpful informants, who at this stage had been joined by police.

I arrested her for attempted murder (after all, why plunge a large kitchen knife into someone if you don't intend to kill them?) The knife was found shortly after, next to a long line of large dustbins on the small service road and was a large black-handled kitchen knife.

Funnily enough, I don't think I was ever called back to the couple at this particular flat ever again!

68.

That Belongs To Us I think

There was nothing remarkable about the type of call; a lone woman had been targeted coming out of a tube station and followed from there by some low life who thought she looked like an easy target. Once down a side road, he had pounced on her, robbed her at knifepoint and got away with some money and her mobile phone. A deeply traumatic event for the lady involved and something she'll never ever forget. If I ever had the opportunity to put all these robbers and burglars into a hole in the ground and bury them, I wouldn't think twice. Pass me the shovel.

She had the presence of mind to knock on the door of a house nearby and they called the police and it was me who turned up. Now if you turn up pretty fast to these types of calls, the suspect must still be around somewhere; they don't just vanish into thin air. I put the victim into the back of the police car and while my colleague was getting the details from her, especially the description of the suspect so we could relay it to other officers, I drove her around the area. It was pretty standard stuff, doing what's called a Street ID. Who better than the victim to identify who had robbed her? Pop her in the back of a car and drive around all the likely areas.

After a while and after slowly increasing our search area (imagine a spiral shape – your search area gets wider and wider as you go around), I saw a lad that fitted the description some way off in the distance and relayed this to other officers. As our distance closed, the victim positively identified the suspect as the one who had robbed her. We don't always find suspects doing it this way, but today was our lucky day. As we pulled up nearby, he made no attempt to run; he just acted as though nothing had happened. Maybe thinking he'd bluff his way out of it, or maybe thinking he was just the subject of a random stop. Yeah right, as if I'd waste my time just randomly stopping people. He was arrested straight away for the robbery and once detained and in handcuffs (all watched by the victim of the robbery – I hope she found some comfort in that) he was searched and the phone was recovered, as well as a knife.

But while searching him, he was found to be wearing some sort of covert body armour, which gives you some idea of the circles these scumbags operate in – he was just guarding against himself being stabbed or shot on the streets one day. Once he was back at the police station and searched further, it was found he was wearing a Metropolitan Police issue set of covert body armour. What's more, there was an officer's shoulder number written on the label and he was one of ours. Some weeks ago some police kit had been stolen from an unmarked car; this item being part of it.

So, he was further arrested for 'Handling stolen goods' then. (No point in arresting him for the actual theft from the car, you'd never prove that in a court.)

69.

Pistol Whipped

A bit further along on the same road as the above robbery (though it must be stressed this was a different day; it's not the Wild West out there), police were called by a passer-by to a man who had been the subject of a beating. According to him, he had been struck around the head several times with a handgun ('pistol whipped' for want of a better expression). Often in these types of cases, you'll never get to the exact truth, or the real reasons that led up to the event. You get one story from the victims, another from the suspects and the truth probably lies somewhere in between the two. I didn't have much to do with the victim in this case; he was being well taken care of by other officers who had arrived on the scene before me. The guy who was beaten said he had been in the local snooker club, had the altercation in there, and was followed outside and attacked.

He was able to give a first name for the suspect, but said that was all he knew. I went along to the snooker hall, spoke to the staff who were working that day and explained what had gone on. I ended up leaving there with the members signing-in book, seized as evidence.

I didn't have much to do with the incident after playing this very minor role in it but was told some time after that the suspect had been identified, helped out in part by his name being in the members signing- in book for the day in question. He ended up with an early morning wake-up call from a couple of ARV units. They had detained him and found a loaded firearm in the flat. He had been charged with various offences including possession of a firearm, and was waiting on his day out in court. Let's hope he got put away for a decent amount of time.

70.

A Doubling Up of Suicide Attempts

You get the occasional person who jumps in front of a train to end their life and you also get the people who slash their wrists. I've seen both more than once. Rarely do you get both at the same time though, but here I was, faced with just this scenario.

The call had come in from the actual driver of the train involved, which is unusual, and reading the copy of the report I have in front of me, the call came in at 7am. Again, an unusual time of day to be called to a suicide attempt I reckon. There were six police units assigned to this call and also the Duty Inspector, probably due to it being at the very start of the shift and it just hadn't got that busy yet.

When we got to the location, which was a level crossing close to the centre of the town, we could all see the man stood right in the middle of the railway line. Because it was on a crossing, the live rails there were covered up of course. We could see the train had stopped a good distance from the man, which was only lucky because the train was slowing to come into the station, which was about 50 yards away from the crossing point. He was holding a knife and had it placed on one of his wrists, although it didn't look like he had cut himself at all. Not up to that point anyway.

A few of us had stepped forward, to the point where the level crossing barriers had come down and met. There were quite a few cars all backed up at the crossing point, all watching to see how events unfolded.

It became apparent that this was more than just a suicide attempt, as the man appeared to be suffering from some mental illness and, as I've said before, there's every chance he can't help what he's doing, or control what's going on in his mind. He wasn't engaging with any conversation, and it was at the point where he just seemed to focus a little too much on the knife he was holding and his wrist, so two of us rushed him and grabbed him by his arms, quickly followed by other officers who took the knife off him. He was handcuffed for his own safety as he was now our responsibility and I didn't want him escaping and doing anything to harm himself. Only once he was secured in the back of a van could you relax a little.

He was sectioned under the Mental Health Act and taken to the local mental health ward of the hospital on our ground, a place some of us regarded as our second home, so much of our time was spent there. He was actually known to them there as a previous patient, as so many are who we deal with. It's like a merry-go-round it seems; they go in, have treatment and then get sent back out into the community again.

I suppose there's only so much medical teams can do for someone I guess.

71.

Another Murder and the First to Arrive Again

This call had come straight from the ambulance service. They had received calls to a male stabbed in the chest after a large fight and were requesting police arrival before they turned up themselves, which is fair enough; they're not equipped to deal with the violence and disorder side of things.

As I got there, I could see it was a large old house that had been converted into loads of small one-room bedsits and I gave the exact location to other officers who were making their way there. There were several witnesses there, all occupants of the other bedsits who had been awoken by the fight. It was about 1am on a Wednesday morning.

As I entered, along with three other officers, one of the people that lived there said that two men were involved and that they had both run off.

As a pair of officers quickly began getting descriptions of these suspects, I went in to the flat with the ambulance crew. Lying on the bed in there and bleeding very heavily from a stab wound to the chest was a man who was around 30 years old. As the ambulance crew did their thing, assisted by us as much as we could, cordons were put into place around the house, crime scene logs started, CID and the Duty Inspector were all requested and attended and other officers began a search for the two outstanding suspects.

The victim was taken out of the house on a stretcher, still being worked on and taken on blue lights to the nearest hospital with a police officer on board for continuity purposes.

The paramedics tried in vain to save the man's life, but during the journey to hospital he went into cardiac arrest and died.

A search of the flat by myself to try and establish the man's details revealed documents from the West London Mental Health Team. This came as no surprise really.

I said earlier that when searching for suspects, they never disappear into thin air; they're always somewhere. One of the officers searching for the suspects decided to widen his search area, and when he was well over a mile away from the murder scene, he saw two men running down a main road close to the centre of town. When they were stopped by him and the other officer he was posted with, they were breathing heavily and sweating. Not only did they match the description of the suspects concerned, it wasn't until they were joined by other officers and the suspects were securely detained, that the officer told them he had seen one of them throw away the knife used in the murder, which was recovered. A great result.

There's a mountain of work following an incident of this magnitude. There's the staffing of all the cordons, the crime scene itself, which includes secondary crime scenes such as where the knife was found and also the ambulance used to transport the victim; that is a crime scene as it may hold forensic evidence from the suspects. Then there's things you might not think of straight away – contacting the council about road closures, the bus companies to get the routes diverted, tracing the next of kin etc., let alone the huge amount of work re: the actual murder investigation.

This one ended up with a trial at the Central Criminal Court, or The Old Bailey as you might know it, and they both received life sentences, which was the best result you could wish for.

72.

How Many Fences Can You Climb in One Chase?

'Yes, a good suspects-on call,' I thought as it came out on the radio. I'd been waiting on a decent one of these coming out and here we were with one only an hour into the shift! Then all of a sudden, as we were speeding to the call, a friend came over the radio who had arrived on scene, stating that there was a ladder up against the side of the house and that he thought it was a workman.

What an anticlimax. I was ready for some fun and games too. Then, within seconds, he came back on the radio saying he was chasing a suspect from the house. Workman my arse, we had a chase going on now with a proper burglar; that's more like it!

The control room had already requested a dog van and listening to my mate who was chasing, the suspect had climbed over a wall into the grounds of some flats and from here over another wall into the back garden of a pub. I arrived at this pub just as my mate was saying he'd now gone out into an alley by the side of a house behind the pub and into a building site at the bottom of here.

As more officers arrived, we attempted to put a containment in around the building site, until an officer said they'd seen him climb from this building site into a small road next door made up of only a few houses. I could hear on the radio as I was running along that a dog van was making its way towards us and that the helicopter had been requested, but couldn't assist due to another tasking somewhere else. It was at this stage that I saw the suspect myself, as he jogged down this little residential road. He saw me and was back over someone's fence yet again.

Other officers had started to try and put in a loose containment around the area, but it wasn't watertight, so I climbed over this garden fence, followed by another officer, only to watch this suspect haul himself up and over another. This went on over another five fences; most we were able to climb over but one we kind of went through instead as it collapsed under us (don't worry, the police paid for a new one for the owner).

In the end we lost sight of the suspect and thinking he must have been in one of about four gardens, we just sat tight and waited on the dog van turning up. It was a chance to get my breath back too. There were other officers who had made their way towards us and they hadn't seen this little shit pop out anywhere, so we were certain he had gone to ground (hidden) in this area. Within about three minutes of the dog van arriving, it found the suspect hiding in an old beaten up shed and in the excitement of it all, it was me who got to him first and nicked him for residential burglary. A cracking way to start the shift off!

73.

The Victim Becomes the Suspect

Now, just because you're a victim of a crime, does not mean you are generally a nice person. Some real thugs can be the victim and sometimes you really don't want to help them, although of course you do. One such example was a man who had been badly beaten outside a branch of a very well-known and popular chain of pubs.

His head and face had been stamped on (later medical examinations showed him to have a broken nose and a fractured jaw) and the fight had been broken up by the door staff there. Police had been called by another one of the customers at the pub who had witnessed all this and quite a few of us put up for the call and attended. Some, including myself, stayed with the victim, created and cordoned off a crime scene such were his injuries, and searched for as many witnesses as possible. Descriptions of his attackers were put out and some five minutes later, I heard that three men had been arrested by a number of officers for the assault, with one still having quite a bit of presumably the victim's blood on his clothing.

This was a good result and the ambulance duly arrived and treated the victim at the scene, before taking him to hospital, accompanied by a couple of police officers. I stayed there at the scene itself with another officer while we waited for the night duty SOCO (Scenes of Crime Officer – the fingerprint lady in this instance), which all takes some time.

Less than an hour later, I heard on the radio that the 'victim' we had been dealing with had refused all medical help at the hospital, had become violent and assaulted three members of hospital staff, including nurses and one of the accompanying police officers.

So now we had three arrested for GBH (Grievous Bodily Harm) on the victim and the victim arrested for ABH (Actual Bodily Harm) on four people who were trying to help him.

I pity the poor early turn CID team the next morning who had to sort out that mess!

74.

Put the Knife Down Mate

A friend of mine on the team was tasked with going to arrest a male on a warrant. Pretty run-of-the-mill stuff; it happens every single day. He was wanted for 'Witness Intimidation and Breach of a Court Injunction'.

He was going there with the officer he was posted with and hadn't requested any help with this, which isn't surprising considering the low-level crime and the fact that checks on the address before he went didn't bring up anything of concern.

It was a different story however when the man answered the door brandishing a large knife and was refusing to come quietly! More officers were requested and I made my way along with a few others. My mate said on the radio that the man could be heard moving furniture behind the front door and thought he was barricading himself in the house. He also closed the front curtains, so no one could see inside.

As officers arrived, some went to the front and some to the rear just to help contain the house. A TSG unit was requested (Territorial Support Group – public order specialists), as they were equipped with long riot shields, should they be needed. We had one of our Robbery Squad cars arrive too, just seeing if they could assist in any way, which of course was welcomed. Any call that has the word 'knife' in it attracts attention from police officers; we even had an ARV unit making its way to us, just as a contingency. Better to have these resources and not need them, than to need them and not have them.

Although the suspect had closed the curtains at the front of the house, he hadn't closed them at the back. Here we heard from one of the officers observing the back of the house, that the male was still walking around inside and clearly had the knife in his hand. It was described as being a kitchen knife with a blade at least six inches long.

On the Robbery Squad was an old school Detective Sergeant, who had around 40 years of police service under his belt. He had managed to engage the man inside in conversation and was chatting to him through the living room window. After a bit of persuasion, the man inside agreed to open the front door in five minutes. Why this amount of time? Who knows, but it was a start at least.

The TSG were some distance away, so there were a few of us there who were public-order trained and had been so for many years. Another officer and I armed ourselves with two long shields from the van and positioned ourselves unseen just on the hinge side of his front door.

A plan of action had been decided upon, where if he opened the door, we would force it all the way open, enter and subdue him quickly, giving him no time to react. After all, he might be thinking the same thing and open the door only to come flying out at us, maybe still brandishing the knife. It's happened before to a friend, who had a kitchen knife thrust into the front of his body armour.

After a bit more conversation with this old school DS, we could hear items being dragged away from behind the front door. As the door catch was turned and the door was starting to open, we quickly pushed forward with the shields, bursting the door wide open. This sent the man inside crashing to the floor, where we pinned him down using the two long shields.

When subdued, he was arrested by the original officer who had gone there to do the warrant, as well as the odd other offence now too! Why people are willing to turn a bad situation into an even worse one I'll never understand. They know they won't win.

75.

Charmed I'm Sure

You'd think that at 4.30 in the morning, you'd be able to wind down a bit from a busy night shift. 'Yeah, I wish.' Sometimes that's when it's starting to kick off, especially when the night clubs start to empty out.

Well one lad had left a night club and decided in his drunken state it'd be a good idea to get in his car and drive off home. That would've been fine, if that pesky telegraph pole hadn't jumped out in front of him, making him crash into it and then send him careering into a line of parked cars.

When we got there, he was still sitting in the driver's seat trying to restart his car. I can't remember who nicked him for 'drink drive', whether it was me or my mate I was with that night, but I certainly do remember getting him into the custody suite. As he got out of the van he tried to run off, but was very quickly stopped; after all, we were holding on to him at the time! Even though he was handcuffed, he struggled and kicked out quite violently, but was subdued before he caused no more than just the few minor bruises and scrapes we suffered.

He was stood up onto his feet and marched through the metal cage of the custody door, but upon reaching there he decided to play up again, pushing himself into us in an effort to escape, which of course wasn't going to happen. He fell forward and smacked the bridge of his nose against the metal edge of the custody entrance cage, splitting his nose open. Served him right and the only thing I was concerned about was that now made the drink drive process that little bit harder to administer.

A dressing was held against his nose, whilst he was held down in a seated position on the bench in front of the Custody Sergeant. He continued with the usual barrage of abuse, calling us every name under the sun, but unfortunately couldn't come up with anything original, which was disappointing.

We were 'all a bunch of white' this, and a 'bunch of white' that; the usual. Like water off a duck's back really. Then the threats start against your families, the 'I'll find out where you live,' etc., and the 'I'll rape your wife while you're at work'. You'd be surprised as to how many times your missus would be threatened like this, almost to the point of it being commonplace. As I said, nothing original to say for himself.

He was charged with 'drink drive and no insurance' or something like that and sent on his way in the morning with a court date. I'm reading all this off of a copy of a Quality of Service Report written by the Custody Sergeant who says himself, the prisoner was the most demanding and exasperating one he had ever had to deal with in his service. If it wasn't for this report in front of me, I'd probably never have remembered it, just another ten-a-penny arrest, but hopefully gives you some idea of what officers have to put up with often on a daily basis.

76.

Sorry Luv, I'll Be Late For The Panto

Ah, Christmas Eve and I had booked off half a day's annual leave to go out to dinner with the wife and two of my kids and to the Pantomime – a Christmas Eve tradition in our house.

I was just booking my vehicle in ready to go home, when a call came out to a serious domestic assault, in one of the tower blocks that overlooked the police station. Good luck with that one I thought, I'm off home. Then there's further info coming out on the radio, that the woman had been stabbed.

Damn, that I just can't ignore, it's just too serious a call. So grabbing the car's log book and keys and my colleague I'd just dropped off, we jumped back in the car and drove around two corners and we were on scene. It was up on the 9th floor of this block of flats and after being joined by another unit we made our way up there. The front door was answered by what you'd describe as an angry chap and we barged our way in, detaining him too in the process. The woman had a severe cut to her shoulder and was bleeding heavily. While a couple of officers attended to her wounds, I arrested him for GBH and I thought 'there goes my dinner reservation'.

The wife of the suspect said he'd hidden the knife behind a picture hanging on their living room wall and as the bottom of the picture was pulled away, out dropped not a knife, but a bloody great machete.

Christ, I think she was very lucky really; she only had 19 stitches at hospital. And you know what? I did of course miss out on my Christmas Eve dinner but just managed to make it to the theatre in time. As we sat down in our seats, the curtain went up!

77.

Stop That Plane!

Not long before I retired, I was out on the airfield at Heathrow Airport, teaching an Airside Driving Course for two new officers on my team.

As we were driving around, we stopped at a crossing point, as coming towards us was a Russian Aeroflot Airbus A330, heading to runway 27R to take off. This would be a good point to stop and talk about clearances between aircraft and vehicles I thought, as the crossing point we were at could be confusing if you weren't paying close attention. The natural area to stop would have been the grassed area in front of us, but if you did stop there, you'd end up being struck by the aircraft's engines as it passed. The very best possible outcome you could get from that scenario would be you going to prison for something like 'Aircraft Endangerment' – the worst outcome would be an aircraft accident, with loss of life. The actual stopping point was some way before this grass area. You definitely had to have your wits about you driving around there, especially at night or at speed should the situation arise.

Anyway, we're talking about clearances and safety as the aircraft taxied by in front of us and one of the lads pointed to the rear of it and said, 'Is that a sticker?'

As I was looking at it too, I saw that the entire rear cargo door skin was missing from the aircraft. You could actually look into the aircraft for a length of about 10 feet and see all the inside structure of it.

As the aircraft continued past us, I called up my control room and told them to get on the phone immediately to Air Traffic Control and to stop this aircraft from taking off, explaining that it appeared to be missing its rear cargo door on the starboard (right) side. This was indeed done straight away and after less than a minute, I watched the aircraft suddenly brake on the taxiway. Airside Operations vehicles started to appear and after a flurry of activity alongside it, the aircraft was ordered onto a nearby stand, followed by various Operations staff and engineers.

We later received a call into the police control room from Air Traffic Control, wishing to thank the officers concerned for noticing the missing panel and for bringing it to their attention. They said engineers were now rectifying the problem. Due to the missing panel being on the starboard side of the aircraft, they said they would never have been able to see it, as they were situated on the other side to it. They also said that the 'defect' could have brought the aircraft down, as high-speed air could have forced its way up and under what was left of the aircraft skin during flight and caused further damage, possibly leading to the loss of the aircraft and all on board.

I bet the passengers weren't too happy though; I kept out of their way!

78.

That Was Some Speedy Arrests

Over the course of two nights, there had been a team of thieves working the arrivals hall at Heathrow's Terminal 5. It's commonplace there for travelling passengers with early flights to get to the airport the night before and find a place to sleep (after all, I've seen some of those hotel prices – they make me sweat just thinking about them) or passengers with later connecting flights the next day etc. There can be literally dozens and dozens of dozing passengers there. They're often a target of bag thieves who'll take a suitcase or similar, hoping to find items of value in them. It's a bit of pot luck I suppose, but I'll never understand the people who leave their very expensive mobile phones on charge and then just settle down to sleep for the night. Would you do that in a train station or a bus station, with people walking around and then fall asleep? Of course you wouldn't.

Heathrow Police have their own dedicated CCTV investigation team and they go through all the crime reports on a daily basis and try to find images of suspects and also to find linked crimes, where it's clear the same suspect is responsible for them. Sometimes, if you've got a really good Evidential Imaging Officer, they'll not just settle for an image of the thief, but track their movements all through the terminal. If they're lucky, they might even be able to see if they used a certain bus to arrive on, or even their car if they've used the car park.

On this occasion, or should I say over two nights, several bags and phones had been stolen. Can you imagine travelling abroad and someone steals your bags, containing maybe money and passports and your phone? What a massive problem that would cause you. God, I hate these low life scum who prey on people.

The CCTV investigator, who was a police officer, managed to track these suspects from the previous two nights and established they were a team of three individuals. They always seemed to wear the same clothing and always appeared to get off a bus (number unknown) at bus stop 6 or 7 and enter through a set of purple doors opposite a branch of a Marks & Spencer food shop. The entrance doors and lifts there are colour coordinated and the purple doors were at the north end of the terminal I think. The CCTV was so clear, it was plainly obvious they had committed the thefts; of that there was never any doubt.

Now if the thefts had happened two nights on the trot, it would be foolish and almost a dereliction of duty to ignore the fact that they might well strike for a third night too, especially as their pickings so far had proved very fruitful for them. A few of us got a phone call at home, before coming in for our night duty shift, to come on duty in plain clothes, with a view to targeting these thieves. It would be us doing it on the first night and then the Crime Squad doing it for the rest of the week.

That night, three of us were handed a little package prepared for us by the CCTV investigator. It listed all the crime reports from the past two nights, suggestions as to where the suspects might appear from and the routes they seemed to take walking through the terminal building. More importantly, it contained still images taken from the CCTV of each suspect taken from different angles, their clothing and bags they carried to blend in, so they looked like travelling passengers themselves (sneaky, eh? I remember when I first joined the police, we had a burglar who used to wear a suit and carry a briefcase when out committing his crimes, crafty bugger!)

We formulated a plan of action, where we'd get dropped off and when, so we'd be in position a good hour before they normally arrived.

When it was time for us to arrive at the terminal, we parked our unmarked police vehicle up and went to walk into the terminal via this set of purple doors opposite M&S. We gave our time of arrival to the police control room, which was met with a 'good luck' from them. As we were walking up to these doors, there was a group of males stood outside waiting to enter, exactly matching the descriptions of our three suspects, right down to the clothing, bags carried and faces. They'd arrived early too.

Now, you could act like you haven't seen them and watch them enter and wait for them to steal again. But

237

this just wasn't going to happen, not an option at all. After all they could have turned around there and then and got on a bus if they got wind of who we were, or we could lose sight of them in the terminal. There was no way they were getting away.

No, we had the evidence already, it was clear-cut, so as we walked past them we turned suddenly and pounced on them taking them completely by surprise, immediately arresting one each, no need for questions and answers, although it was explained to them why they were being arrested obviously.

The time between us giving our time of arrival and then asking for transport for three bag thieves, was about 90 seconds according to the report at the time. Now they were some speedy arrests.

They were all charged with the thefts from the two nights before and after a lot more CCTV investigation, also charged with a further six similar offences from the month before. And custodial sentences were later given to all three.

A very satisfying night's work.

79.

Urgent Assistance? No, Just Me Making an Arrest

Just on the subject of bag thieves, a call came in to the police control room of a bag theft from a Canadian family in the arrivals hall of Heathrow Terminal 3. The woman calling was saying her daughter's suitcase had just been stolen, well within the last 5 or 10 minutes she reckoned and she was saying that there was a CCTV camera right above where they had been standing.

The police CCTV operators kept a radio in their office and they were on it like a shot, as a couple of us made our way to the location.

Now, there's no point everyone going straight to the victim in cases like these: one unit can. Everyone else can start a search for the suspect – he's around somewhere. The CCTV operator only had to backtrack a matter of minutes, so the suspect was quickly identified by them. He was described as a man with short dark brown hair, wearing a dark brown 'bikers' style jacket, covered in zips and studs and blue jeans. The jacket sounded distinctive, but don't forget, they can always ditch any item of clothing they've got on. It's why sometimes when you're getting descriptions, it's good to focus on things that can't be easily changed – facial hair, trousers and shoes especially. But let's face it, most victims of crime remember the big things like jackets and such, and it's perfectly understandable and reasonable why they do of course.

There is a tube station in the centre of the airport and this is where I went, along with a good mate of mine to try and find the suspect. They'd nearly always come in and out via the tube or a bus.

While going there, information came out over the radio from the CCTV officer that the exact suspect for this theft did the same thing the day before. However, on that occasion, the owner of the bag saw the theft and tried to wrestle it off the suspect, only for the suspect to punch him in the face, breaking his nose. He had run off with the bag too, so the poor guy who got hit didn't even get his bag back for his efforts. So he's not only a bag thief, but it would appear a violent robber now too.

One of the officers, who was now with the lady victim, informed us that the stolen suitcase had her daughter's name written on the side of it, 'Newman'. Also, the CCTV operator told us that the suspect did indeed walk down towards the tube station, but had also walked back up from the tube station, but couldn't add anything further at that stage.

Anyway, we walked down onto the tube station platform that takes people away from the airport back into London.

There was a train there already waiting to leave and the staff delayed it a few seconds while we quickly looked in through all the windows. No bag-stealing robber in there.

As the train left, we both stood behind one of the wide concrete roof supports, thinking we'd hang around for a while. Almost in that instant, popping out into our sight from behind a large advertising hoarding, came a man wearing blue jeans and a brown biker jacket with zips and studs on. And what was he carrying? A suitcase with 'Newman' written on the side of it.

Now, to say I pounced on him might be a bit of an understatement I think. While I was grabbing him and arresting him for that bag theft and the robbery and assault the day before (and very probably telling him exactly what I thought of him) my mate was on the radio straight away, saying one arrested, transport required etc…

The control room responded, asking us if we required 'urgent assistance' as they thought we were in a violent struggle with the suspect. 'No' said my mate, 'That's just Keith nicking him and telling him what he thinks of him!' He got a good jail term for this, I'm pleased to say.

80.

Taser Him Now!

I honestly can't remember why we had to arrest this guy, but arrest him we had too. I think he was wanted by the courts on a no-bail warrant for something. He appeared high on drugs, had been drinking too and just to make matters that bit worse, he was a very big bloke, tall and very overweight. Oh, did I forget to mention he had his 11-year old daughter with him, that he was clearly in no fit state to look after?

All the ingredients were there for it to kick off, no matter how carefully we trod. And kick off it did, quite literally actually. A few of us had turned up and despite a bit of diplomacy (you can't reason with a drunk who's also drugged up), he wouldn't listen and tried to push us aside and walk off. We grabbed a hold of him in an effort to not let him walk off and he swung around fast and started to throw his arms around to strike us. He was forced onto the floor, where we tried to secure him.

Now, his poor daughter was witness to all this, and she stepped forward and started (understandably) to repeatedly kick me, shouting to let go of her dad. One of the other officers there just held her back; after all, I couldn't blame her for defending her father – I'd probably do the same!

It was a struggle to try and get his arms free enough to handcuff him and at one point he very nearly managed to clamp his teeth on me. In fact, I think it was the only time I've ever come close to being bitten by someone. It's always something you're aware of and guard against, but not this time. We had just fallen over at the right angle for him to be in a position to do this. He was desperately trying to bite me. I had my Taser on me (Did you know it stands for Tom A. Swift's Electric Rifle? Some old story from last century? I digress…) but I wasn't in a position to use it, so I blurted out to my friend, 'Just Taser him!' Which he did.

We were in such close proximity to one another, rather than just shoot the suspect normally with it, bearing in mind we were a bit entangled together, he quite rightly took the cartridge off the front of the weapon, exposing just the electrodes and pressed it against the man's back. Now, using it this way can be seen as a 'pain compliance technique' and should only be used as such if you can really justify doing it. After all, we're not there to torture the guy, just to stop him hurting me. The Drive Stun only lasted a second or two (proved in the subsequent Taser download), just enough time for me to get myself out of reach of this guy's mouth. He was arrested for whatever he was originally wanted for, not the subsequent struggle. That was just part and parcel of him not wanting to come quietly; some fight back against arrest, most don't. The daughter was returned to her mum about an hour later by other officers.

The man ended up making an official complaint against us, about the way he was arrested and especially the tasering. It was all investigated by Detectives from the Serious Misconduct Investigation Unit (SMIU) and it was concluded that we had no case to answer. In fact, we received an email from the senior investigator, praising us for the standards of our 'highly detailed and thorough statements,' saying that if our standards could be replicated throughout the Met, he'd be out of a job.

Praise indeed, you don't often get it.

81.

A Critical Time-Sensitive Arrest

There can't be a crime that is as repulsive as that of an indecent assault on a child. Especially when you find out that it has been going on for some time.

The call to one of the airport terminals originated as simply a female crying and staff at the location couldn't get anything out of her at all, so they had called the police.

When I arrived, I was met by an elderly Chinese lady, who was crying inconsolably. She had a flight ticket on her that, according to staff, had been purchased that very day, which seemed odd. Normally people have booked their return tickets well in advance; it's a little rare that they're bought on the day of departure. She seemed genuinely relieved upon seeing a police officer. Now that's not always the case with people from China; they're just a little suspicious and intimidated by their own police back in their country it seems. Several times I've smiled at people from China whilst patrolling in uniform and carrying firearms and the look of surprise on their faces always makes me laugh, and they nervously half-smile back, while acting very shocked that they'd met a 'friendly' police officer.

The woman's English wasn't that good, so I managed to find a Chinese member of staff who was willing to interpret for me. No matter the nationality of the person you're dealing with there, there's always someone around at an airport who can speak the language concerned. Now this lady lived in China and her daughter and granddaughter were over here living in the UK. Her daughter had recently married an Englishman she had met over here and they were all living together somewhere in the Birmingham area. The husband of her daughter was not the child's father.

This Chinese lady had noticed that her granddaughter was very withdrawn and not herself. She also seemed very quiet when her stepfather was around. It was during a conversation she was having with her granddaughter, who was 10 years old, that she had managed, in between tears, to tell her that her stepfather had been touching her where he shouldn't.

What hit me for six though, was when she told me the granddaughter had said to her, 'Sometimes he puts his willy in my mouth, and I can't breathe'.

She had angrily confronted her son-in-law about this, while her daughter was out at work she said. He had become enraged, packed up her bags himself that very morning, bought her a flight ticket home and driven her down to the airport and dumped her off there. She was crying inconsolably because she didn't want to fly back to China knowing what she knew and just didn't know what to do or who to turn to. All this was explained to me through a lady acting as my interpreter don't forget.

That was it, this guy was getting nicked come what may, even if I had to drive up there myself and do it in my own time. I brought the Chinese lady back to the police station and went and saw my Detective Inspector, a close friend I'd known for 25 years. It was decided to interview the lady and get all her statement and allegations recorded on tape. While a Chinese interpreter was being contacted to come to the police station to assist in this, a couple of Detectives from the CID were tasked with the interview.

In the meantime, I contacted West Midlands Police and managed to speak to an Inspector from the area where the family lived. After carefully explaining what we had discovered this end, thankfully they seemed as keen as me to get this male arrested, before further harm could befall this child.

As soon as the interview was over, I was to contact him on a phone number provided so they could continue with the investigation their end.

This I did and the last I heard a few days later, was that the stepfather had been arrested the very same evening that they had received the allegation. That's the last I heard about the case; I had no more involvement in the investigation.

It was now in the hands of West Midlands Police. If the allegation was true and I certainly had no reason to doubt it, I hope he got all that was coming to him. And a bit more.

82.

An Easy Arrest for a Change

'Don't go out thieving wearing your work uniform' would be a better subject heading I think. The call was to a branch of Dixons, the electrical retailer, based in the airport. Staff had noticed that one of their laptops had been stolen, but this wasn't discovered until the next working day.

They had reviewed their CCTV themselves, saw who did it and called the police.

When I went down there to view the CCTV myself, I saw that there were a few customers in the store at the time and one of them carried a large broadsheet newspaper under his arm. He simply placed the newspaper over one of the laptops on display, unplugged the alarm cord to it, which luckily for him didn't appear to go off and walked away with the laptop, carried out under the newspaper. So simple.

Although he was wearing his own jacket, he had a very distinctive tie on. I recognised the tie as one certain members of staff wear, staff who work for Heathrow doing customer questionnaires. Also, he appeared to be in his late forties, a white guy (that's relevant) and had greying hair.

Now that was a starting point. If he was a member of staff, he'd have an airside pass. Any door that he had exited out of would record his pass being used. Utilising our own CCTV operators back at the police station shortly after, I was able to quite accurately guess the door he would have exited out of, when we tracked his movements after he had left the shop. Also a rough time frame. I drove back to the terminal building and found this door and noted its number. All the doors there have their own individual numbers.

Armed with this information, I popped along to the Heathrow ID Centre, who issue all these airside passes to staff, and had a word with one of the managers there. I knew him already, as I'd done this same sort of thing before to identify a couple of men for burglary and fraud. He was more than willing to help because who wants a thief in their staff?

Using their computerised system there and knowing what door he had used and at roughly what time, it showed that about 80 staff had used the door 15 minutes either side of the time frame I'd given him to check for me. He simply eliminated from the list on the computer screen all the females and all the Asian names. This left a list of about 20 people and he went to bring them up on the screen one by one.

The very first one that came up on the screen was our man, absolutely no doubt about it. We got his name and address, etc., and checks showed he hadn't used his pass that day as yet. Every chance he was still at home then.

He was living locally and within about 30 minutes we were outside his front door. I knocked on it and he answered, and it was 100% the same man from the CCTV. I said that we were there about the theft of the laptop from Dixons and he denied all knowledge. I said how I'd got perfect CCTV of him stealing it and I explained to him how he'd done it. He said, 'It's in the living room. I'll go and get it'.

Such a simple job, it just shows that if you've got a little bit of info to start with, with a little bit of digging around you can often get your man. He had his airside pass seized from him and ended up losing his job over it, as well as a day out in court.

He pleaded guilty of course.

83.

Tastes Like Chicken

While patrolling around in the early hours one morning just as it was getting light, I came across a Caribbean restaurant that had had its front door smashed in, with glass lying everywhere. This was just on the edge of a large dodgy council estate that I might have mentioned before.

There was a chance someone could be inside, so getting another unit to join me, we climbed in through the hole in the smashed glass door and searched inside. There wasn't anyone in there, probably just some drunken idiot in the night getting angry and kicking the door.

But when we went downstairs, we saw there were a couple of large cooking pots simmering away on a very low heat on the large double ring cooker. The original slow cooker it seemed.

Piled up high on the worktop there, were a load of dead pigeons from the estate, all waiting their turn no doubt for the cooking pot.

And my wife wonders why I don't go into these backstreet fast food places!

84.

At Least Someone Noticed

It's always incredibly sad when people die and they're not missed by anyone. There's no one to raise the alarm like a family member or a concerned neighbour. Once I went to a 'sudden death' as they're generically called, to find maggots actually wriggling out from under the door. The downstairs neighbour had only called us because a dark patch had been getting bigger on his ceiling down below.

Another was to an elderly lady who had collapsed or had fallen down the stairs it seemed. This call came from the postman who had noticed her letters piling up in the front door letter cage on the inside. I had broken into her house via the back door and found her at the bottom of her stairs. Now, a warning, pass this bit of you're squeamish – she was badly decomposed and the smell was out of this world. Her whole chest area and face and neck pulsed up and down with the amount of maggots heaving in her. She was so close to her front door, I had to stand astride her to unlock the door to let my colleague in, stepping on the occasional few maggots as I did so.

The poor old love. She's probably someone's mother and grandmother, who knows what she had achieved in her life. I clearly remember a very old and tatty black-and-white framed photograph on her sideboard, that I presumed was of her. She was absolutely beautiful.

Now it's quite common, if you can't get hold of any next of kin, to do a search of the house to see what you can dig out. By this I mean address books, phone books, etc., just to try and trace a family member or even a friend who might know of any relatives. While looking in her cabinet though, we found £14,000 in cash. Obviously she didn't trust the banks it seemed! All this was seized, as it was too valuable to leave there and you wouldn't want it to go 'missing' and then for a family member to allege that police had stolen the cash. I've seen that happen before.

One time I forced my way into a house because of a suspected collapse and the person inside was lying dead, close to their five-bar electric fire and they'd literally been cooked like a burger on one side of their body. Not good.

Another time was to an elderly lady's house, where we could get no answer at the front door. The neighbours were certain she was inside and offered me the use of their ladder to get in through an open upstairs window, fearing she had collapsed inside as she was apparently very frail. I climbed up the ladder and slowly started to search around the upstairs of the house, peering around every door frame fearing my gaze would be met by some rotting corpse.

As I looked around a bedroom door, I could see a dark dirty pair of feet sticking out from under the bed covers. As long as I live I'll never forget the really long curled dirty toenails. I pushed my head further and further into the room, looking further and further up her body, until I got to her face. She had one of her fingers rammed right up her nose, having a right good root about in there for something that wasn't coming out easily. She saw me and let out a loud scream, matched in volume only by mine I think!

One collapse I was called to involved a man I knew well. He was probably in his mid-forties and known to the police for a huge variety of crimes. I think I'd personally arrested him maybe two or three times. He was a violent individual, who had beaten his wife before now, and beaten and robbed his elderly neighbours in the flats where he lived. All in all, a nasty piece of work. When I arrived the ambulance crew were trying to resuscitate him and inside I was dying to tell them to stop. He would have been no loss to society. But his wife was present and whatever happens there's always that duty of care and saving of life that always comes first. He was taken to hospital anyway and I stayed at the flat with his wife – I can't remember exactly why she didn't go in the ambulance with him. Presumably because they were still performing CPR on him and that's not always a good thing for a family member to witness. It was while I was driving her to the hospital a short while later, someone who was there with him said the male had passed away and gave a doctor's name and the time he had pronounced life extinct. Just after that information had been passed on the radio, someone, I don't actually know who, but they obviously had prior dealings with him, gave a cheer over the radio. Luckily, it wasn't noticed by the wife.

85.

Show Me Unavailable for the Rest of the Shift

Now how the hell did I get to arrest three people for three separate offences in the space of about ten minutes? The first was a result of a call to a small estate after midnight, where a boyfriend (ex now!) had forced his way in through the front door to his girlfriend's house and had ended up punching her in the face. A few of us had turned up and I'd nicked him for assault. He had been put in the back of a van and as we were driving out of the estate and on to the main road, some idiot had come tanking it around a corner in his car and had hit the kerb, before coming to a rest against a lamp post right in front of us. I had leapt out of our van and ran over to him, to find him quite obviously drunk and dazed, sitting in the driver's seat wondering what had happened. He was nicked for drink drive by me and rather than put two prisoners in the back of a van where anything could happen between them, especially as one is pissed and one is angry and violent, we called up for more transport.

Now as we're waiting on a second van to come and lend a hand, a short distance away around this very same corner, along comes some guy riding a bike. He sees us and thinking we hadn't seen him, he gets off the bike and chucks it in a front garden hedge of one of the houses there. As he casually walks past us, I lean out, grab his arm and after a few questions I nick him for theft of a cycle.

Blimey, never again. To say I was busy trying to sort that lot out would be an understatement. I know a few people chipped in to help out though. Must have been when I was super-keen and dedicated to the job!

86.

A Calming Hand

'A 17-year-old male with mental health issues smashing up the house' was exactly how the call came out over the radio. I was with one of my Sergeants this afternoon, who quite liked to get out of the police station every now and then and 'blow the cobwebs away' so to speak. We took the call and as we were approaching the house, we saw two people come running out of the front door as fast as they could. They saw us and ran over to us as we got out of our car. It was the lad's mother and a care worker from the local council. The funny thing was, the first words blurted out from the very upset and crying mum's mouth was, 'Please don't hurt my son'.

'Er, I've got no intention of hurting anyone,' was my first thought!

There was a lot of screaming and hollering coming from the house and before I could utter a single reply to the mother, a large wooden drawer unit was thrown out of the closed front ground floor window, like one of those scenes from a western where someone is hurled out of the saloon windows during a fight.

The window glass and bits of the frame shattered all over the front garden and then a few other smaller items started to get thrown out too. There was screaming coming from inside still and as I jumped up onto the front garden wall to look inside the room, my Sergeant said not to go in there, but to wait until other officers arrived.

When I looked inside the front room, there inside, cowering in a corner was a young lady, who happened to be a second care worker. The other care worker had somehow forgotten to tell us that when we arrived.

The young lad in the address was known to the local Mental Health Team and lived at home with his mother. He was visited every so often by a couple of care workers, presumably just to check up on their welfare and to address any concerns or needs they had. But on this occasion, something had snapped inside him and he had gone into a rage.

There was no way we could wait for anyone else to arrive; that young care worker in there was terrified and no doubt fearing for her safety. We had to get in there and fast.

The front door was open, but the hallway was full of broken or upended furniture. There was a wardrobe lying broken on its side, a table and some broken chairs. We climbed over all this and went into the living room at the front of the house. The lad was still in quite a frenzied state, with his arms outstretched and yelling at the top of his voice. The room had been trashed and the care worker was huddled up in a corner of the room, with her arms clutching her legs into her body and her face pressed tight against her knees for protection.

I put my hand on to the lad's outstretched arm, expecting a bit of a roll around, but he just turned his head, looked at me and lowered his arms. It was like flicking a switch; his whole demeanour changed in an instant, so I got him to sit on the sofa in the room, while my sergeant got the poor care worker up and out of the house, before coming back to me.

The lad had suffered a few cuts to his hands and arms from all the broken glass and while I gently spoke with him, I began to clean these up. Eventually he was taken to hospital to get checked over, accompanied by another police officer.

Sometimes the police being present in certain circumstances can exacerbate someone's behaviour and sometimes it can help draw it to a calmer resolution. You just can't tell in advance.

A nice result from this was the letter of thanks we received from the lad's mother. Maybe she appreciated our tact and diplomacy, when she was expecting something more towards the other end of the scale? You've got to tailor your reaction to what's in front of you and be able to modify and adapt it, as and when circumstances change. Sometimes it's obvious you've got to go in hard straight away, but sometimes you don't have to at all.

It's a judgement call at the end of the day, down to each individual officer's interpretation of events they're presented with. Most officers up and down the land make these judgement calls on a daily basis and let's face it, they usually make the right ones.

87.

A Hospital Perv

Now this poor elderly lady we were called to was Iranian and was an inpatient at a big London hospital. She only spoke Farsi, which wasn't ideal, but had managed to convey to a nurse there the fact that she had been indecently assaulted overnight by another one of the hospital staff. This nurse had discussed it with her ward manager, who had ended up calling the police and it was me who turned up to deal with the allegation.

When I spoke with the lady, it was clear that there were language communication issues between us. This allegation was far too serious to investigate with just a bit of pidgin English or the help of someone local there who spoke the language, so I called my control room and arranged a Farsi interpreter to meet us at the hospital. This took a couple of hours to sort out, but once they had arrived we could begin to investigate appropriately.

After the usual introductions, we made sure she was comfortable explaining events to me. She was, although understandably a little embarrassed by it all. She went on to explain that over the past three nights, a member of staff had come up to her in her bed, slid his hand under the covers and indecently assaulted her. She had been ashamed by what had happened and no doubt was in a state of shock too. It seems this third assault on her had been too much (as if the first one hadn't) and she finally found the courage to tell one of the nurses what had happened and they in turn had called the police.

A long trawl through the CCTV with hospital security (they're never too good at operating their own systems) showed one of the hospital porters entering the ward at about the time the lady said she was assaulted and leaving shortly after. He wasn't actively working it seemed, not wheeling patients around or anything like that, and when we saw him on the CCTV entering the ward on the night before too, that was enough, especially as he matched the description given to us by the lady concerned. We got his details from one of the hospital managers and went to his home address and nicked him on suspicion of indecent assault that evening.

This was all handed over to the CID to investigate further and we just went on to the next job. I'm not too sure what the outcome was at the end of the day, but some time later we did get a handwritten 'thank you' letter from the lady's daughter, thanking us for our 'sensitive and considered approach', which was nice. It certainly makes you think that what you're doing, and your efforts, are appreciated and are worthwhile.

On the subject of indecent assaults, another springs to mind. One night duty we had been dealing with a horrendous sexual assault that happened on a lone female in a park, where several lads, who weren't even known to the victim, had pinned her down and penetrated her with a large stick they'd found close by that had broken off a tree. Can you imagine the sort of sick bastards that do that to a woman? Some had been arrested by officers and it had obviously been an incredibly harrowing ordeal for the poor girl.

I dealt with her and didn't actually have any contact with the suspects whatsoever, as you certainly wouldn't want any allegations of cross-contamination of evidence when and if the case came to court. You want to make sure you do everything possible to help the victim. Actually, thinking about it now, it's probably a good job it wasn't me who arrested them. You're always professional of course, but some crimes and suspects certainly do test that fact. I believe this case did get to court, but I wasn't required to give evidence in the proceedings. I do know that some or all of them got prison sentences though, which hopefully was some comfort to the poor girl.

88.

Ghostly Goings-On

Not so much a funny story, more of a ghost story now. On one of my old grounds I used to work on, there was a well-known house removal company based there, whose main premises was a very large old warehouse-type building. It had been built on the site of an old World War One ammunition factory, so the owner told me, and this building there now dated back to the 1960s.

Anyway, very early one morning we received a call into the station about the building's burglar alarm going off, and a couple of us made our way there as quickly as possible. When we arrived, I could see that one of the ground floor entrance doors was wide open, but with the building being so large and with so many places for anyone to hide inside, we just secured it from the outside by putting a containment in (putting officers on two opposite diagonal corners so each can see down two different sides of the building), and requested for a dog unit to attend, which they did.

I knew one of the dog handlers who had turned up, and after a quick briefing as to what we had, they went inside to start their search. It was while they were inside that the keyholder turned up. (The keyholder is simply the person who the alarm company has on their system, who they phone up in the event of their alarm going off, so that they can turn up with the keys etc. to sort the alarm out).

I explained to the chap who'd turned up what was going on, and while we waited outside he told me a little about the history of the building. He also explained to me they don't let staff work in the building alone, and no one ever works there at night. Obviously this leads to the question of 'why'? He said that as it's mainly a storage type building, there are a lot of metal staircases and metal walkways around it inside. Often, he said, 'staff hear the sounds of someone running up the staircases, and also walking or running along the walkways inside, when there's no one there'. 'It freaks them out a bit,' he said, and most staff had experienced it. 'It's why no one works on their own in the building, it's all just a little unnerving'. As I said, it was a large building, and wasn't attached in any way to another, so there was no sound transferred from one building to the other.

Fast forward maybe 15 or 20 minutes, and the dog handlers came out to meet us. We don't tell them what the keyholder has said to us, it's back to the job in hand. They could find no evidence of a break-in, and everything inside seemed undisturbed, so that was all good. 'What was strange', said one of the dog handlers, 'was the dog had detected someone behind a closed door' he said. The handler had opened the door, and made repeated calls for the person to show themselves, or he would send in the dog. There had been no reply, so he let his dog off the lead, and it ran towards the corner of what happened to be an empty room. He explained his dog was going crazy, reacting to something in an empty corner of the room, and it wouldn't stop or return to him upon his commands; it just barked and snarled wildly, and was shaking with his hackles all up. He said he'd never ever seen his dog behave in that way, ever, and in the end he had to put the lead back on the dog's collar, and literally drag it, still snarling, out of the room, as it continued going absolutely wild towards what was just an empty corner. It was then we explained to the dog handler what the keyholder had told us, and it made the hairs on the back of all our necks stand on end!

That reminds me – a few days later I was working nights, and I was parked up in the yard of this same removal company's building, telling the ghostly story to a friend of mine I was posted with that shift. After I had told the story, all the lights around the building and those illuminating the yard suddenly turned off, plunging the area into complete darkness. I've never driven out of anywhere so fast in my life!

That building has been knocked down for some time now, and standing on the site at the present time is a large development of very nice posh flats. I've always wanted to speak to the owners of those flats, and just ask them if they ever experience any ghostly goings-on? I don't think I'll be buying one anytime soon!

89.

Stabbed in the Back, Quite Literally

This was a call to yet another man who was quite well known to several of the local officers. It had all started a few years back, with police being called to the house because of arguments between him and his wife as the relationship deteriorated. They both seemed as bad as one another really. Both a nightmare to deal with in the way they wound one another up, especially if we were there.

Over time the arguing and threats had escalated and despite the wife being offered help several times with ending the relationship, it just wasn't going to happen. 'But I love him' is the reply you often hear. It's understandable to a degree, they've had years invested in each other and money tied up in the house, but luckily in this instance no kids to witness their arguing and fighting.

It was after one of these times that it had escalated that the husband had been arrested. Not by me, but I heard he had been sentenced to a couple of months in prison. I had nothing to do with that job. I guess this time she had had enough and was willing to press charges for some assault, as she maybe could see this wasn't really the best relationship she could be in.

When the call came out on the radio this time, the 999 operator had stated that there were sounds of a large disturbance in the background.

When we arrived at the house, you could hear the fight going on from out on the pavement. There were high pitched screams of 'Leave her alone' coming from obviously a third person in the house and the screaming of another woman. It was kicking off big time and after a few thumps on the front door and the shouts of police, it wasn't being opened. The fighting sounded like it was coming from just the other side of the door, so fearing for someone's safety in there we had to get in fast, so one almighty kick of the door just by the latch sent it bursting open.

It was a momentary image I saw that I'll never forget. I can picture it perfectly in my mind's eye right now.

The wife was lying face up on the stairs in the hallway, fighting off her husband, who was lying on top of her, pinning her arms back, while he had his teeth firmly clamped down on one of her exposed breasts, as he literally bit a chunk out of it. In that very same instance the other woman present, the wife's sister, plunged a small kitchen knife right into the man's back screaming to 'Let her go'. All this was seen in the tiny fraction of a second it took us to leap forward from the front door to the stairs and grab hold of him.

It turned into a proper fight for a few seconds between him and the two of us; he was on another planet with his level of violence. He just managed to break free from us (it was a bit crowded at the bottom of the stairs with five of us there) and ran out of the back kitchen door that was wide open, with us after him, right on his heels. He was grabbed and wrestled hard to the ground, ending up with us rolling around in a thorn bush. He was handcuffed after a properly violent struggle and I arrested him for GBH. Job done.

The wife ended up needing surgery I seem to remember, but for the life of me I can't remember what happened to the wife's sister. I'd guess nothing, as self-defence is the best defence you can have in those circumstances.

I do remember though, he'd only been released from prison that very day. I wonder if they could've reserved his old cell for him?

90.

That's All Folks

Every day in the police you're dealing with something. Far too many different things to ever remember. Friends have spoken with me, saying 'Do you remember when we did this or that?' – and no, I don't! They told me about many robbers and burglars we've chased, but nope – don't remember that. Maybe a very vague fleeting recollection is there, but no more than that at best really.

I've mentioned arrests and suchlike in here, but you deal with so many you'll never remember them all. The most arrests I've had in a week was eight, the most on one shift, as I mentioned, was three. What has been written about here is only the tip of the policing iceberg that I remember, and what has been written about on these pages are incidents that I have dealt with personally. Nothing here was dealt with by other people, or were jobs I was just on the very periphery of.

I've always had friends and colleagues with me of course, it's ALL been one big team effort, everything has.

There's just so much more I could mention, but on their own they just don't warrant a story.

I once told a friend to always bring your grub out with you on a night duty, as you might not get the chance to go back for it. He didn't bring it with him that night and within the hour we were first on scene where a young lad had been shot in the stomach. That took up the whole shift (It's OK, I shared my grub with him).

I've been working on the front counter at police stations too and had my fair share of fun and games there – arresting many people over the front counter and once or twice seen mentally ill people put their head through the glass windows on purpose.

I've had a live hand grenade put on the front counter, even a lost tortoise (he's still in my back garden all these years later after the RSPCA couldn't rehome him). I even found a great big crab once walking, (or is that scuttling?), down a residential road in London. He was rescued and later put into the nearby tidal part of the River Thames.

It may sound like an urban myth, or some old wive's tale, but along with a member of the public, I've actually rescued five ducklings that had fallen down a drain near to the Thames, while the mother duck watched and quacked loudly nearby!

I've chased squirrels out of an old lady's house and even changed smoke alarm batteries for another. I've fallen asleep at the wheel of a police car right on a bend in the road and ended up nose first in someone's allotment, after first introducing the front of the car to a couple of trees. I never actually got in any trouble over that either. The Garage Sergeant turned up, expecting me to say a black dog had run out in front of me or something, but I just admitted to a 'micro sleep' on the bend after a busy Friday night duty shift. He was fine with that. He just said to go as a passenger for the next two night duty shifts, and start driving again on the Monday late turn. Honesty does pay, see?

You see so much death it almost becomes mundane, but of course it never is. I've sat in houses where in the same room sits the deceased, still in the chair that they died in. I've been at a death where the elderly partner of the deceased is in such a profound state of grief that the officer I was with started crying too. I'll never forget that one actually, as the poor elderly man we were dealing with pointed to his clock on the mantelpiece that had stopped, he said, at the same time that his wife passed away. I've dealt with so many suicides I've lost count. From hangings to overdoses and even twice to carbon monoxide poisoning suicides, where they have had a pipe leading from the exhaust into the car. Even had a guy who had slashed his own wrists while lying in the bath (that was a strange one, as I clearly remember his cat coming into the bathroom while we stood there, stopping at the door threshold, arching its back and hissing loudly towards the bathtub. Obviously sensed something).

I've chatted to Presidents, Prime Ministers and Hollywood A-listers, as well as extremely senior members of the Royal Family – I even tried to get one of the Royal Family to buy me a tea once and when they said they had no money on them I accused them of having short arms and deep pockets, which we all (including them) had a genuine laugh about.

Many's the time I've used a prisoner's own jacket to mop up the spit they've left in a police van while they've watched - (they don't like that, but guess what – unlucky). I even used a man's jacket once to clean a police car after he pissed against it one night. Once I talked a guy out of suicide after he'd doused himself in petrol and was holding a lighter.

Another time, whilst patrolling in plain clothes in an unmarked car with a colleague, there was a bit of road rage between the drivers of the two cars queued up in front of us. The driver of the leading car got out with a hammer, and started smashing up the car in front of us. He got the shock of his life when he was grabbed in no uncertain terms by us and swiftly nicked.

You deal with all sorts as time goes on. Looking at my HR record I had printed out before I retired, the amount of injuries sustained whilst on duty ran to four A4-sized pages. Everything from smoke inhalation while searching for people in a burning flat, to lacerations requiring stitching up at the local hospital, to broken bones, and seemingly endless cuts and bruises from violent offenders who didn't want to come quietly. I've been spat on so many times I've lost count. Several times I've been called to large fights, or come across them in the street while being on my own, and you can't just wait for others to arrive to assist you. Sometimes, you've just got to get stuck in. I remember the time I came across a big fight outside a taxi office involving about seven or eight people late one night when I was on my own. Getting in the middle of that to try and break it up resulted in several of them turning on me. Didn't end too well for me that night, that's all I'll say about that.

Above all, whenever I've been dealing with any incident really, I've often thought – if I told my kids what I'd done, would they be proud of their old man and think, 'Yeah Dad, well done!' I do hope so.

Some of the incidents mentioned have resulted in the presentation of a variety of commendations, presented to me by various Chief Superintendents, and even the Commissioner, and also awards from the Royal Humane Society for life-saving. But you know what? Nothing beats knowing that you can count on your mates to be right by your side when it's all going bent. That's what it's all about. That's the greatest reward there is.

I hope I've been a good copper; there's certainly parts I really miss. The people that is, not the work. If anyone is reading this who wants to join the police, I'd say go for it. You'll see things other people rarely, if ever, get to see. You've got to have a degree of empathy, understanding, compassion and discretion. A strong stomach might come in handy too.

Buckets of common sense and a hatred of criminals who prey on the vulnerable are the real essentials though. After all, it's police work, not social work.

As a great copper once said to me when I was young in service, 'Bear malice and take it personally and you'll be a better copper for it'.

Amen to that.

👁 👁 keep 'em peeled

Printed in Great Britain
by Amazon

15748407R00166